It was good enough for Father

Ruth Wilkerson Harris

It was good enough for Father

The story of the Wilkerson Family

Fleming H. Revell Company
Old Tappan, New Jersey

Scripture quotations in this volume are from the *King James Version of the Bible.*

To the memory of my father,
whose faith still inspires those
who sat under his ministry.

Preface

COMING FROM a family of dreamers, I did my share of dreaming as a young girl. Although I outgrew fantasy in my teen years, I still clung with fierce tenacity to three of my childhood dreams. The one I liked best was that of marrying a Boaz (as had the Ruth of the Old Testament), the second was to be an educator and the third to become a writer.

This book about my family fulfills the last of these dreams. Realization of a dream is seldom an exact match of the fantasy. My Boaz turned out to have very little of the world's riches, but he does have a measureless wealth of understanding of the needs of others. I am not that great educator, but I have many opportunities to teach the Word and participate in vital Christian education.

During my husband's early years in the ministry, my thoughts of writing about life in a preacher's home remained a dream. I was engrossed in helping to dig wells for country parsonages, painting church walls and visiting prospective members. Through the busy years of raising four children, there never seemed to be time for writing, but the dream was still there.

When my brother David became an author, it seemed to me that the glorious happenings in his life were all the more reason for me to write about our heritage.

John Adams, writing in 1775, expressed my inspiration. "To look back and recollect the adventures of myself and my family, [and Grandfather and his family,] I see a kind of romance, which [without] any embellishment of fiction would equal any thing in the days of the [Old Testament Patriarchs] or the [Apostles]."

RUTH WILKERSON HARRIS

Contents

It was good enough for Father

1

The Pioneers

Patriarch Wilkerson obeyed with faith when he was called from England to go out into a place named Tennessee where he was to receive (for a small price) a plot of America's frontier land. He sailed across the waters, not knowing where he would arrive.

Being a romanticist, I'd like to brag that our adventurous forefather arrived on the "Mayflower," but alas, I must confess I was unable to trace the date or place of arrival. It can be presumed from the scattering of stories handed down that his arrival was probably in the early eighteen hundreds.

"It's just as well you don't know," this generation of Wilkerson adventurers tells me, "you'd only want to brag."

"Sure I would! Just think—us poor, uneducated, former across-the-tracks religionists suddenly discovering ourselves related to someone famous!" I was getting warmed up to the idea when Mom's stern voice cut me short.

"Listen, my dear, it doesn't matter who you are related to, or how much learning or wealth you might acquire. When you stand before God, you'll answer only for yourself."

"You know I'm aware of that, Mom." I answered sheepishly, "but still . . . " I can never keep from dreaming!

I suppose the greatest natural heritage we Wilkersons received from our courageous ancestors was the spirit of adventure and the ability to visualize what at first may be a dream but may become a reality. So if any member of our family tree has accomplished anything of importance, it certainly isn't to our own credit.

Our forefathers were not among the number of Englishmen hoping to get rich fast in a growing county. They had a dream born out

13

of their love for God. For years the Wilkersons belonged to the Church of England. Somewhere along the line they joined with other dissatisfied church members who felt the Church had never made a complete break with the traditions of the Roman Catholic Church. Calling themselves Baptists because their distinctive belief was in baptism by immersion, they braved the religious intolerance of their day and formed another church. In America there was an opportunity to escape ridicule and even physical violence suffered because of their acts of "heresy."

The decision of my family to settle in Tennessee more than likely was prompted by a land company in our great-great- grandfather's home town in England, that happened to be selling plots in the Blue Ridge Mountain area. The choice of such mountainous terrain far inland is typical of my family's decisions. One of my pet gripes is, "Can't we *ever* do anything the easy way?"

I can't be hard on the first of the Wilkerson pioneers, though. I'm sure they found it necessary to join hands with a group of like believers who felt it safer to settle in a relatively unpopulated part of America. That assured them a secluded place of freedom to worship and immerse as they pleased.

History verifies that they weren't settled in America long before the War of 1812 broke out. This is where I must dream! For our illustrious grandfather (past two greats) joined the forces of a local Tennessee officer by the name of Andrew Jackson. He was wise enough to know only a free country could offer freedom of religion. So off to war he marched!

Romantically speaking (and I do believe it is true), our American forefather became friends with Andrew Jackson. They both lived in the same area of Tennessee. Jackson, appointed prosecuting attorney for the state, then elected senator, then judge of the state's superior court was a farmer hewn from a rugged mountain way of life and would certainly have been in contact with his fellow farmers.

"Do you realize," my dear impudent husband had the nerve to point out, "your illustrious ancestor might have met Jackson when he was hauled into court for a violation of the law?"

"And would my illustrious ancestor have named his son after Jackson had your presumptious theory been true?" I asked triumphantly.

"Maybe he was acquitted by Judge Jackson!" One can never win with a stubborn Welshman!

The Wilkerson portion of America, located sixteen miles outside of Knoxville, prospered into a reasonable facsimile of a farm. The log cabin progressed to a wooden frame house of several rooms and later to a large two-story southern home. The hilly countryside was dotted with farms owned mostly by Baptists. In the midst of their community stood a small log church, the focal point of all their social activities. Religious freedom, with a definite Baptist slant, abounded in these secluded mountains. The Wilkersons were happy to be part of it—happy to be Americans.

When a son was born in 1845, they proudly named him Jackson in honor of President Andrew Jackson. It was evident he had inherited the same adventurous spirit of his father. Young Jackson felt his heritage and name destined him to follow in the footsteps of his father. And this is where I can brag!

Soon after the Civil War broke out in 1861, there was once again a Wilkerson defending his country. Tennessee was one of the last states to secede from the Union. There were few large plantations and few slaves in East Tennessee and that section remained strongly Unionist in sentiment during the war.

Jackson Wilkerson joined the Volunteer Army of Tennessee when he was only sixteen—just the age for excitement—and he was itching to become a hero. His aging father didn't share the same enthusiasm for his young son's aspirations. (He forgot his own adventurous spirit stirred up his son to follow in his own footsteps.)

My father often would tell us we came from the line of "Johnny Bullheads." He was impressing us that a Wilkerson never gives up. He neglected to add, they often never give in, either. Jackson's persistence showed he had inherited both stubborn qualities.

No amount of pleading moved my great-great-grandfather. Steadfastly he refused to give in to Jackson's begging that he sign for him. Neither did he give up trying to persuade Jackson to wait until he was eighteen. He hoped the war would be over by then.

Jackson never ceased pleading with his father for permission to join the army and finally settled the argument by running away. The Wilkerson men were tall and he easily passed for eighteen. Thus, Private Jackson Wilkerson was duly inducted into the service of the Union Army in 1861, swearing to God he was of age, and was

15

assigned to Company A, 2nd Tennessee Infantry.

Not many months later he became Prisoner Wilkerson in his own state for defending his state and made prisoner by his own countrymen for defending his country by virtue of the divided loyalties within Tennessee.

"A sure sign of the end times." his father shook his head. "Why, it's brother against brother: our freedom is gone, and only God knows whether we'll ever have peace again."Jackson's prison days held no excitement, at least not the kind he had been seeking; but he did experience adventure—of a sort.

When the prisoners found themselves without water, Jackson remembered his father's method for solving problems. Since it worked for his father, he saw no reason why it wouldn't work for him too.

So Jackson prayed a simple prayer: "God, we need water. You promised to supply our needs without exception. Now I'm asking you to show me where I can find water in this prison camp." Then he waited for the answer.

One of the striking traits of the Wilkerson men was, and is, their simple trust in God. I've heard stories, like this one of Jackson, and I have seen situations in which most Christians would either succumb or entirely give up: yet to my family they have become challenges and chances to prove God honors the faith of His children without reservation.

That night Jackson dreamed a dream in which God revealed to him the exact spot where water ran below the earth's surface. Early in the morning he took his tin cup, and while others guarded, Jackson dug until water bubbled forth.

He was most happy to share his bounty with his fellow prisoners, but never let it be said a Wilkerson refused to make use of natural talents. Jackson had dreamed other dreams in that prison. Back home a young lady was waiting for her hero and Jackson envisioned a golden opportunity to insure a *yes* to his marriage proposal the minute he got back from the war.

His "store" flourished; it seems no one could do without his commodity. So across the counter came the coins to fatten the groom's purse. The soft spot in his heart allowed the poor to drink freely, but, oh, how the rich did share their wealth! It's amazing Jackson survived. I guess his likeable personality covered up for his lucrative business venture.

16

The Civil War ended in April of 1865. Jackson was not freed until a few days later when news of the truce reached the camp. On the thirtieth of the same month, Jackson and Sarah Jane Lynch Selvidge were united in marriage.

Together they set about doing their part in planting and replenishing the war-torn state, and, in more ways than one, they were successful. Sarah worked side by side with her husband, mending fences and barns along with planting until things were back in order. Then they began an extended program to enlarge the population of Knox County.

Into their brood of eleven children came a handsome baby whom they patriotically named James Arthur Garfield in honor of the twentieth President, James Garfield and his running mate, Chester Arthur. He captured the spotlight from the moment he was born and never stepped out of it. He became my grandfather.

The only permanent tragedy that marred Granddad's entrance into the world was his father's choice of name. Unfortunately, this presidential name had catastrophic influence on Granddad, causing him to commit deeds quite unpatriotic.

Had his father lived to tell Garfield the stories of his part in the Civil War and the stories of *his* grandfather's exploits, then possibly Grandad would not have taken such a dim view of his name. But our great-grandfather, his health greatly affected by exposure to prison with lack of food and medicine, could not survive the struggling years of establishing a fruitful farm. He died in 1881 at the age of thirty-six. This left Granddad, only two then, with just his big brothers and his fist to defend his honor and his name.

His older brothers, long since over the sting of being called Yankee-lovers, only laughed when they saw their younger brother getting all worked up over insults hollered back and forth by the young Confederate crowd. So it didn't take Granddad long to learn how to come to his own aid without the help of unreliable reinforcements.

"Hey Garfoot," the more prosperous sons of neighboring farmers would call. "What's the son of a Yankee-lover doing livin' down in Rebel country?"

"You call me that name again and I'll punch your nose flatter than a buttermilk biscuit." Granddad wished he'd hurry up and be "grow'd up" so he would be able to carry out his threat.

That day finally came. Soon there wasn't a boy in Knox County who hadn't felt the affects of Granddad's threats.

He listened to a dozen or so versions of his illustrious name and flattened not a few noses before reckoning that it just wasn't worth doing something for his country. Someone else would have to promulgate the name of his father's favorite president. From then on, Granddad became known by a variety of names, but never again would he acknowledge the name of Garfield.

Although Granddad could not see being so patriotic as to shame a son with so Yankee a name as his, nevertheless, he was proud that his father had fought for what he believed. Even though they were poor, they were clean, respectable and religious, and his mother taught him that was all they needed to walk with their heads in proud equality with the wealthy—even the Confederate wealthy. Granddad wore his Yankee heritage (minus his name) like a flag, waving it in the faces of his enemy. After all, he figured, being the son of a Yankee put him on the winning side.

With a quick fist and a sure-fire line, he learned all by himself how to settle the war still being waged by neighborhood kids, and somehow he managed to stay on the winning team the rest of his life.

Hearing stories of Granddad's life, I'd say he was kept on the winning team thanks to the women in his life. I can't determine who had the greatest influence, but there's strong evidence his mother knew how to keep young "J. A." walking the straight and narrow path as long as he lived at home.

When his father died, Granddad quickly learned that he had to accept responsibility even at his young age if the Wilkerson family intended to stay together. Mother Sarah wasn't about to give up just because her husband died leaving her with eleven children to raise.

One of the first things she did was take advantage of a government pension her husband had earned by serving the Union. This allowance wasn't much, but it kept them decent people. Sarah was too proud to beg or borrow from any of their relatives, so she rallied her eleven assets around her and put a work plan into effect. She enforced a work schedule, defying anyone of her brood to disobey her orders, and that included the youngest—Garfield!

Stories of the generals her husband and father-in-law had served under were at last worth all the patience she had mustered in listening to them told over and over. With Spartan-like tactics, she maneuvered her small army into accomplishing feats that most Southern women left to hired hands. From morning to night she issued orders and like a good "general" she led her army through each accomplishment. There were no slackers on the Wilkerson farm.

Sarah was up before dawn to light the fires and to prepare hearty breakfasts for her children. She woke the older boys first and, after feeding them a large portion of the food, she sent them off to the fields. An hour later, the younger children were roused. The girls were allowed to finish out an entire term of school, but the boys had to break off their schooling for the planting seasons. Because Granddad was only two when his father died, his years of schooling numbered even fewer than the other boys. He was needed badly on the farm after his older brothers married and left to build their own homes. Granddad left school at the end of fourth grade with no intention of taking instruction from a schoolmarm again.

Being a dropout at the age of nine never seriously affected Granddad. Granddad's theory—experience is the best teacher—served him well in making some of the most important decisions of his life. Granddad wasn't averse to book learning, but it was many a year after the day he closed the door of the little one-room school house in the Tennessee mountains before he was convinced he, J. A. Wilkerson, needed more schooling.

I don't know how much reading and writing Granddad learned in four years, but he never had trouble matching wits with anyone he met, either in business or in the ministry. I suppose his mother made sure her children could read and write about their Yankee-flavored heritage.

Of course, Granddad couldn't sign his full name, but only because he made up his mind he wouldn't—not even for Uncle Sam. If people couldn't call him "J. A." (Jay), they needn't call him anything.

By the age of nine, he did excell in at least one subject and that was farming. His mother saw to it that he got all the experience needed. Sarah and her little "army" became quite successful farmers. In fact, it wasn't long after her husband's death that she was able to buy a more prosperous farm. Her early morning drills, her instructions for precision planting and a constant watch over the fields yielded abundant harvests. Granddad bragged all his life about the hundreds of bushel measures he filled with green beans. They sold in the Knoxville markets for the great sum of twenty-five cents a bushel.

19

Weekly market trips permitted an ofttimes overworked crew a chance to expend their pent-up energy. I suspect Granddad enjoyed many of his early experiences on these trips with his brothers. Their escapades rarely met with the approval of their "Company Commander," but Sarah knew better than to take on boys six-feet-plus, even if they were her own sons. She needed their cooperation, not their rebellion.

When her children reached the age where she could no longer use the rod, Sarah applied her own homespun philosophy. Granddad told a story (with noticeable satisfaction bordering on the worst of the sins of saints—*pride*) about his oldest brother, Will, being cured by one of his mother's remedies. According to Granddad, Will was the sneaky one of the bunch. He had a girl who lived several farms away and every Friday night he would get slicked up for his date. No one could vouch for the time of Will's return, but Granddad was positive it wasn't the same night. Since Will couldn't do without his sleep, he was forced to sneak a few winks between plowing fields. Those quick catnaps often lasted through the morning, and soon Mother Sarah began to notice the fields just weren't up to par.

"Now what do you suppose a general like my mother could do with a great big fellow like my brother, Will?" Granddad would ask, his eyes sparkling with mischievous glee, as if seeing it happen all over again.

Sarah knew better than to lecture, and she certainly couldn't "court-martial" Will. She needed his service if she could still get it out of him. She pondered the situation for awhile, keeping the others in suspense as to how she would punish the big brother.

Sarah said not a word. That evening while the children slept, Sarah got out a clean pair of underwear for Will and neatly laid it out where Will would easily find it and be sure to put it on—but not before she rubbed the inside with hot pepper fresh from the garden.

In the morning when the younger boys left for the fields, Will, wearing his clean underwear, sleepily followed them out. About high noon, Sarah left the house for an inspection tour. She headed right for Will's territory. Just as she suspected, Will had found a comfortable spot to sleep.

"Only he wasn't exactly napping," Granddad would say with a roar. "There he was, the hot sun burning him up, but not as much as that hot pepper! Why, he squirmed, he scratched, he rubbed and

20

he swore, but nothing stopped Mother's home remedy from doing its job."

Just then Sarah came out of her hiding place and gave poor Will a lecture like he had never heard before and hoped never to hear again. Will was in no position to disregard his mother's warning.

Granddad told this story with great relish because he felt himself too much a man of wisdom to get himself into such a position as Will. He was too busy living to sleep away his life. Occasionally, Granddad took time off from farming to see the world around him. On one of these trips he discovered the square dance and the fiddle players. "I took a hankering to music, bought myself a mandolin, sat on Ma's front porch and learned to play." It was as simple as that with Granddad, when he wanted to do something. Before long his Saturday nights were taken up with playing at the square dances.

Every Saturday night, Granddad put on his only suit, pressed to perfection, his only white shirt, starched so stiff it could stand alone, slicked back his black wavy hair with the latest brand of hair oil and took off down the road with his mandolin under his arm, whistling the hit dance tunes.

"James Garfield." Granddad stopped suddenly in his tracks; he was sure he heard someone call him by "that " name. Who'd dare, he wondered. He looked beyond him, trying to pierce the darkness. Not a soul was in sight. Thinking he had only imagined the voice, Granddad started off again, only this time a little more cautiously. "James Garfield," the voice came distinctly. Granddad stopped with a jolt, his hair standing on end, and swung himself around with fists ready to strike, but no one stood ready to charge. Through the eerie quietness came the voice: "Garfield, I want you to preach the Gospel." The voice came from above.

Granddad was more annoyed than relieved to know it was a message from heaven. Calmly he pushed his waves back in place, picked up his mandolin from the road, stood his full six-feet-two-inches, looked up toward the star-filled sky and in firm tones said: "God, I'd rather die first." Hoping this was his final contact with God about such nonsense, Granddad stalked off, still whistling and anticipating a great deal more excitement than what had just been offered him.

Now Granddad didn't doubt for a minute that the voice had been

21

God's. His mother had brought up each one of her children in the knowledge of the Lord. While the boys were young, they took delight in following behind their mother's steed as she rode sidesaddle to the church, but as they grew older they thought themselves too manly to be tailing after a woman to attend Sunday school. They declared that it was for women and children anyway. Naturally, young J. A. chose to be manly, too, so his church days ended not long after his school days. Though Sarah couldn't force her boys to church, they had to take part in family prayer as long as they lived in her home. It was enough to keep the spark of faith alive in their hearts.

So Granddad readily acknowledged that he'd received a "call" —yet the idea of exchanging his fun-loving way of life for a pious dignity that seemed to be a trademark for all the parsons he'd ever met was unthinkable. Once Granddad let God know where he stood, he simply forgot God's proposition and went on his merry way. There would be a time when he'd remember this call.

For Granddad that night, the more important voice came from a petite Southern belle named Della. With her dark brown eyes she had looked up into J. A.'s twinkling eyes and, right on the spot, Granddad boldly informed Della, "We're going to get married." Della had come to the square dance out of loneliness; she was only sixteen and already she had to make her way in life. Meeting a tall, dark and handsome "feller" who wanted to marry her seemed like a page out of a storybook.

Granddad had been thinking for some time about marriage. At sixteen his alloted money had been cut off, and he knew he must soon find work since his mother could no longer support him. Thoughts of going off alone didn't appeal to him at all. He liked the woman's touch, especially since he preferred to remain ignorant about such things as taking care of his clothes, cooking a meal or cleaning a room. By nature, Granddad liked people. Crowds were his delight and he liked being in the middle, dominating the conversation.

Granddad's proposal was sealed in 1900. Under a cherry tree on a lane in Knox County, Della and he exchanged vows for the circuit-riding preacher. Granddad worried not a minute about the responsibility he ardently assumed as husband at such a young age. No challenge bothered Granddad at that moment of his life. For that matter, no challenge ever seemed too great for him to accept.

22

Granddad had an indomitable will to *do*, even if *doing* didn't please anyone. As long as he thought it the thing to do, then he did it, and that was it. Somehow it usually turned out *to be* the thing to do.

Mother Sarah wondered if getting married was the thing for her youngest son to do. She couldn't imagine mischievous Garfield settling down to become a husband and a father, but Sarah under-estimated her son's five-foot, fiery-eyed bride. Della promptly took over where Sarah left off. Granddad surprised the whole family. In less than a week, the bride and groom were living in Knoxville and Granddad had a steady job delivering ice. The real shock came when they heard J. A. attended church regularly with his wife. Sarah was assured now that her youngest would turn out all right. For all she knew Della might even persuade Garfield to answer the "call."

2

Operation Granddad

GRANDMOTHER said she married Granddad for two reasons; first, because he was a good Baptist, and second, because he was tall, dark and handsome—and in that exact order. She wasn't ashamed to admit she had lost her heart, but she wanted to make it clear to her debonair husband that she hadn't lost her religion.

Della Kytz, orphaned as a young child, had been raised by her grandfather. In the few years he lived, he made it his responsibility to see that his granddaughter was well versed in the Scriptures. He died when she was eleven, leaving her with friends who continued to lead Della in the ways of the Lord. Tragedy deeply etched the message of God's love on her heart and mind. To her, God became a father, a mother, a sister and a brother all rolled into one, and no man, not even the handsomest fellow of Knox County, could steal her cherished faith. Serving God was Grandmother's way of life.

"This is the way it is, dear; God first and you second." There was no other way with Grandmother. She assumed that was the way every married couple lived; so, of course, she expected Granddad to agree readily with her theory.

It didn't take her long to learn that with Granddad it was Wilkerson first, wife second, friends next and somewhere, anywhere he could fit it in, was God's place. With Grandmother that would never do! Steps had to be taken to show her husband the error of his way, so Grandmother got together with God and laid plans to snare the soul of J.A. Wilkerson from the tempter. It took a bit of doing, but the end result was a triumph of one woman's faith in God.

After Grandmother's discussion with the Lord about her husband's religious status, she rested on the promise that the prayer of a righteous woman availeth much. Grandmother saw no reason to consider herself other than righteous.

Even her parson had words of praise for Della's faithfulness: she never missed a service, her good deeds were known by many and she had that rare ability of being a cheerful giver. Grandmother was upright; there was no denying that point. Her example before her husband was above reproach. This, thought Grandmother, would surely influence J.A.'s transformation.

She was pleased when Granddad readily agreed to attend church with her. In fact, it annoyed her to discover he knew just as much about the Word as she did, and she couldn't understand why it didn't affect her husband in like manner.

"If you know so much about God, why isn't He the most important person in your life?" Grandmother would ask this question almost everytime they came from a church service. "Don't you feel God there?"

"Oh, was He there? Where was He sitting?" Granddad liked to tease her just to see her dark eyes flashing with fire.

"James Garfield, don't be sacrilegious! God might strike you dead for your sinfulness." Now Grandmother was angry!

"Well, Della, if it's the truth you want, it's the truth you'll get! No! I don't feel God there. It's the same thing Sunday after Sunday, and you might as well know I only go to keep peace in the house. Why, there's more life down at the Odd Fellow's Hall than in your church."

Grandmother was too upset to speak. It seemed her plans were backfiring, and she had tried so hard to win her husband to the Lord. For some reason she had failed and her sincere distress was more than she could bear.

On her knees she confessed her blunder to the Lord. Forcing her husband hadn't done one bit of good. "So now, Lord, you do it your way," she prayed.

God had His own plan. It had been in effect for a long time; even Grandmother wasn't aware of His ways. But at last she stepped out of the way long enough for God to get things done.

"Operation Granddad" began on a warm summer night. Grandmother talked him into going for a walk, "Just to cool off, dear."

In the center of the town they came upon a group of men and women holding some sort of meeting. Granddad had a nose for anything religious; he could detect a church meeting a mile away. He jerked his wife's arm to steer her in the opposite direction, but already her ears had perked up at the sound of voices singing hymns.

Excitedly she tugged on her husband's coat sleeve, pulling him through the crowd right to a prime spot in the front row. Grandmother was in seventh heaven. She stood as if in a trance, completely enthralled by the enthusiastic singing and testimonies of salvation and healing. Her husband's mounting aggravation went unnoticed. Fidgeting from one foot to another, Granddad frantically sought a way of escape.

"Clang, clang," down the tracks came the Main Street trolley. Granddad, imprisoned on one side by a wall of saints and attracted from the other side by one of man's latest mechanical wonders, momentarily had thoughts of taking a freedom ride. "Hey, Wilkerson," the motorman shouted above the singing. "What are *you* doing with *that* bunch?" and he let out a loud guffaw pointing his finger at the gathering. Being forced by his wife to be a reluctant bystander was mortifying enough, but now to be found guilty by association was too much for my proud grandfather.

"My God, Della, let's get out of here." He got a good grip on his wife's arm and forced her to keep up with his long strides until he had assumed a safe distance. Sweat poured down his forehead. Loosening the stiff collar around his neck, Granddad heaved a loud sigh of relief, "Now that's all I'll hear down at the barn in the morning."

"James Garfield, what do you mean by pulling me away when I wanted to listen. There's nothing wrong with those people. They were only trying to tell about the wonderful things God has done for them." Thinking of the glorious testimonies she had heard dispelled her indignation over Granddad's display of bad manners. "Why, I think it's marvelous. Oh, how I'd like to testify like they did. We never hear anything like that in our church."

"Thank God for small favors." Granddad mumbled his selfish prayer to himself. He hoped his wife would forget this rude interruption of their peaceful walk, for Granddad felt his wife's present religion sufficient for all evil. For her to get any more religious would put him in a bad light: he reckoned he had enough to gain him entrance through Heaven's pearly gates and made a mental note not to take a stroll on a Saturday evening.

26

Granddad had underestimated his wife's religious longings. Her love for God and desire for a more meaningful faith made her want to know more about a religion that still taught about miracles. Not for one minute did she forget the words of the testimonies she had heard that early Saturday night.

Grandmother didn't know she had come across a turn of the century happening. Revival fires had been sparked in the late eighteen hundred's by church members concerned for the growing coldness of their churches. Some groups felt their churches were in a back-slidden condition condition because of the lack of holiness in the membership. Ministers began pounding away at the sinfulness of the people. Clothes, hair, worldly goods and a host of other outward "sins" became the targets of this new emphasis. It never occurred to them that *Ichabod* might be written above the doors of the sanctuaries because of their failure to recognize the rightful position of the Third Person of the Trinity. Other groups felt they lacked the power of the Holy Spirit as promised by Christ to the church, and they sought for the Spirit to come upon them as He had in the days of the Apostles.

Religious writers and theologians, some of them Pentecostal, have tried to pinpoint these particular revolutions within the church, but exactly when, where and how they happened, I don't believe anyone can say. The far-reaching and lasting results of these moves could have been only the work of the Spirit within people scattered throughout the world.

Grandmother's inquiries the very next day revealed the folks holding the street meeting were from a Wesleyan Methodist church. They were most happy to have her join them in prayer. "Our ladies meet in each other's homes every day for prayer, why don't you come?" Grandmother accepted the invitation without a moment's hesitation. Already, in her heart, she anticipated new blessings from God.

She returned from her first prayer meeting overflowing with joy through her first contact with women who could pray the prayer of faith. She couldn't wait to share this news with her friends. It was too good to keep to herself. She told them: "Before, I was religious, but now I've found real faith."

"An overdose, if you ask me," her friends whispered behind her back. They had a lot of love and respect for Della. She was a good Samaritan if there ever was one. They didn't mind her sharing her delicious home-baked bread; but seeing her tuck a Bible under her arm on her missions of mercy set their tongues wagging. Grandmother's venture into faith became the highlight of the women's sewing circle.

The attitude of her church saddened Grandmother, yet she wasn't about to give up faith she knew to be real just because they refused to acknowledge that miracles could still happen. She gave notice to the church clerk: "You had better give me my church letter before I'm asked to remove my name from the rolls."

As Grandmother grew in the knowledge of a New Testament faith, she was astounded to learn revival was spreading throughout the United States. All churches were being affected, but denominations as a whole went on record as stating that it was only an emotional demonstration put on by the uneducated and the poor folks. Glibly, they backed their theory by declaring the Acts of the Apostles were not for the modern age. "God doesn't work miracles in our day as in the days of the early Church," pastors scoffed from behind pulpits, and the majority of congregations believed them.

This didn't stop members from leaving their historical churches and joining thousands who sought a deeper spiritual experience. The very idea that God would pour out His Spirit again was based on the Word. "And if God is the same yesterday, today and forever," they reasoned, "then why wouldn't He continue to endue His church with power?" These earnest seekers combined their prayers, unaware that they were laying the foundation for a body of believers who would someday be referred to as a third force in present day religion.

Grandmother's powerful Gospel was not forthcoming from the Pentecostals, but from a group seeking holiness. Their adherence to a strict code of ethics, morals and rules regarding outward appearance made them an oddity even in that day. In spite of their idiosyncrasies, they stood out as shining lights in a world filled with atheistic beliefs and churches that were distracted from their first love. The skeptic onlookers had to marvel at the simplicity that produced amazing results; town drunkards were saved, people were healed of all manner of diseases and wayward sinners cried tears of repentance.

All except one wayward saint!

When Grandmother came home with her newly acquired faith, her husband just pursed his lips as if in deep thought, shook his head as if in disbelief, and then shrugged his shoulders and dismissed his wife's announcement from his mind. But not for long! When Della Kytz got an added dose of religion, she expected her husband to receive also.

But Granddad had inherited a religion from his parents and they from their parents. "If it was good enough for my parents, it's good enough for me." What he really meant was that he was satisfied with his present religion which didn't require too much of him. He was sure that ignoring Grandmother's latest religious fad would dampen her enthusiasm for an evangelistic campaign to change him.

He was wrong. All Grandmother would talk about was her new faith. Granddad decided to try his powers of reasoning. Now my Granddad was known for his own brand of highly successful phsycology. He was a man of rare qualities, capable of a blunt diplomacy but void of real tact. Granddad approached his wife with his gentlest tone, "Della, we aren't bad people. We went to church every Sunday. If it's prayer meetings you want, why can't you have them with the folks of our church? *We* can always use a bit of prayer."

Well, Grandmother had deliberately set out to break her proud, stubborn and arrogant husband, and she didn't plan to do it diplomatically. Not for one minute was she fooled by her husband's smooth approach. No doubt it was that reference to the *we* that gave Granddad away.

With much righteous indignation she attacked Granddad's false piety; "Goodness won't get you into heaven; and if anyone could use a bit of prayer, it's you, James Arthur Garfield." That double insult (Grandmother only called him by those names when she was angry), was enough to break off diplomatic relations as far as Granddad was concerned. Now he would face her with the truth!

"Half the town thinks you've gone crazy, Della." He wanted to add his own feelings about his wife's present sanity, but from experience he knew better than to incur her wrath. "For the likes of me, I don't see why we have to change. If you want the town to think you've gone batty, don't get me mixed up with such hogwash. I'll be damned if I ever join a bunch of idiots!"

"If you had any kind of religion you wouldn't be cursing, James Garfield. You don't have religion, you just go to church so folks will think you're respectable. I know you, and I say *you* need religion!"

29

Her accusations were like adding kerosene to the fire in a pot belly stove. "Don't you start your holy religion on me. I've got all I need." Granddad emphasized his not needing any more religion with a crash of his fist on the kitchen table.

Grandmother added a bit more fuel to her already blazing husband: "And if you had any kind of a religion you wouldn't be showing your nasty temper."

"What temper!" Granddad's explosive shouts echoed through the neighborhood. Grandmother already had slipped quietly out of the kitchen. She had made her point, now she intended to take her problem to the Lord and to the ladies' prayer meeting.

Granddad set off for work, slamming the door behind him and muttering he'd never change his religion for a bunch of emotional, overwrought so and so's.

If rewards were given out for stubbornness, my grandparents would have tied each other for first place. Granddad meant what he said that morning just as much as Grandmother did. The battle charge had been called, the enemies had taken their positions and only surrender on the part of one of the sides could end the war. Grandmother had no thought of weakening. She had Someone fighting her battles!

But for Granddad nothing was going right anymore. Finally, out of desperation, he sought the advice of his own minister. He didn't want his wife to know how much her prayers bothered him, so he took off from work one day, hired a horse and buggy and traveled sixteen miles to the church of his youth. He felt sure his old parson would tell him how to handle his fanatical wife and settle this infernal dispute about religion, thereby ending his misery.

Granddad got just the answer he had been hoping for: "Son, don't you worry about Della; she'll get over her passing fancy. And don't you worry yourself about your religion. We all sin a little everyday. Now you go on home and act as if nothing happened."

Granddad had reached the point where he'd heed any advice or accept any morsel of assistance in his battle. He was relieved to hear his sins wouldn't keep him from entering heaven's gates but he doubted his parson's idea that his wife's new religion was a passing fancy. To go home and act as if nothing happened—why, the look in Della's eyes blasted that theory! The sound of her praying told him if he didn't get away from his wife, he'd surely succumb to her wiles.

In those days Granddad had a job that was of some prominence in Knoxville. He operated a trolley for the City Traction Company. It seems Granddad had formulated his own plan for exacting fares from people who thought the city should provide free transportation. The open-sided trolleys gave riders a good opportunity to carry out their beliefs, so to his always immaculate uniform, Granddad added a small black, pearl-handed pistol, in full view of his customers. It never failed to bring results. As a reward for his "bravery" the company promoted Granddad to motorman.

The most popular trolley in town happened to be Granddad's. He welcomed his passengers aboard, especially the ladies, as if they were boarding the Presidential Car. He kept their minds off the jolts and bounces with highly fictional stories of his youthful escapades. Granddad became the hero to the children while the adults sat back listening with amusement to his endless stories of pranks and heroism.

Granddad's exuberant personality wasn't getting him anywhere with his wife, though, neither was his fussing and fuming about her religion. His only relief from her persistence was to stay away from home as much as possible. The trolley barn, a popular gambling house, became Granddad's hangout. His new-found friends soon convinced him he needed their fellowship, so he joined the Odd Fellows. Granddad's deeds brought much sorrow to Grandmother; still, she trusted God, praying: "Lord, bring my husband to you at *any* cost."

To make matters worse, Granddad's conscience bothered him. His wife's prayers brought back memories. After his job in the ice company, he had decided to work in the mines. This work didn't appeal to Granddad, but it paid well. On one of the mornings he was to do down into the mine, he woke up to the loud ringing of the alarm clock. The clock stopped abruptly, seemed to dance right off the dresser, smashing into a dozen pieces as it hit the floor. Grandmother took this as a bad omen and begged Granddad not to go to the mine. For some reason, he listened. Early that afternoon an explosion ripped throught the mine, killing almost every miner in the area. Granddad's work in those mines ended after he had spent several days helping to rescue the few men still alive. His conscience pricked him that day—he wondered why God had spared him. His thoughts were troubled with the memory of that

31

night when he was only sixteen and had dared to say: "God, I'll die first."

Granddad's brushes with death seemed to be God's method of constantly reminding him of his call. He left the mines with a hacking cough that reached the critical stage of pneumonia. The doctor gave no hope for his recovery. Only the prayers of his wife saved him, and he knew it, though wouldn't admit to it. Now, constantly standing while operating the trolley, he developed enlarged veins in his legs and not even the rubber stockings that he wore faithfully would relieve the aching.

Not long after Grandmother prayed for his salvation "at any cost," Granddad had his third bout with death. Even Grandmother became alarmed. "Lord, this isn't what I meant," she informed God. But God knew the way to Granddad's heart.

The news from Dr. West, family physician, wasn't good. He told Granddad: "J.A., you've got galloping consumption and there's not much I can do for you. Your only hope is to move to a drier climate."

Granddad just couldn't bring himself to believe the doctor. "It will wear off. I'm strong. I'll outlive Doc."

Secretly, he wished for even a portion of his wife's dedicated faith, but he was too proud to admit he needed God and too proud to identify himself as a sinner. His stubbornness had a price tag, too. His left leg had become so stiff he could hardly move it, his stomach so full of ulcers he could not eat a full meal and his constant cough left him in a weakened condition; yet he rejected the prayers of his wife to settle his account with God, still searching for another remedy.

On the advice of a friend who was a Bible professor, Granddad began to use a remedy of corn whiskey and rock candy. It was just a little at first—enough for his stomach's sake—but soon he found he needed about a gallon a week to satisfy his desire.

This new remedy showed no signs of improving Granddad's physical condition. In fact, it only worsened his faltering spiritual condition. It took all the grace of God for Grandmother to live with him, yet her faith stood firm. She had prayed that prayer and meant it. She only wished the cost wouldn't have brought her husband to his present state. Grandmother never knew in what condition Granddad would come home. Often it was in a drunken stupor, causing the devil in him to lash out at his wife and her religion.

He relented of his evil deeds almost as soon as he committed them and tried to make amends with peace offerings, the last of which was a beautiful sixteen-ribbed umbrella. It must have been before Grandmother was sanctified. As he was about to hand it to her, she swept the umbrella out of her husband's hands, shouting: "James Garfield, the Bible declares it is better to obey than to sacrifice," and proceeded to break the gift over his head. Never again did Granddad bring home a peace offering.

Grandmother believed a price must be paid for everything in life —the greater the value, the greater the cost—so she was prepared for the shock of having her husband leave the family. His excuse was to get into a better climate, but his real desire was to escape the prayers of his wife and her fanatical religionists.

Little did he realize those very prayers followed him every mile he journeyed to Danville, Illinois. All the devils in hell couldn't stop Grandmother's prayers from reaching their destination. It took only three weeks for God to bring about a confrontation between Himself and James Arthur Garfield Wilkerson. That's how long it took Granddad to make the decision to attend his first holiness service.

A tent meeting in the nearby community of Georgetown was the current attraction when Granddad arrived in Danville. He had no intention of attending, of course, but it seemed the entire population was going for one reason or another, so Granddad, curious by nature and having nothing better to do, made his way to the Nazarene tent revival one night.

Granddad entered the tent cautiously. He fully intended to play the role of critic and was looking for a good seat from which to view the "show," when a young fellow, smiling from ear to ear came up and grabbed his hand.

"Welcome, brother." Granddad thought his arm would shake off. "Here, let me find you a good seat."

Granddad was about to inform the kind man he wasn't his brother, but already he was being pushed firmly down the aisle to a front bench. He was too weak to resist, and no sooner was seated than another "brother" approached from the front and thrust a paperback songbook into his hands.

Then a voice boomed through the tent: "Everybody lift your voice to God and SING." And did they sing! Granddad was quite unprepared for such goings on. Forgetting his role of critic, he listened in spite of his arrogant intentions. Granddad talked about the first holiness sermon he ever heard for many years afterward.

The text was Matthew 5: 29,30. Plucking an eye out and cutting an arm off seemed terribly harsh words for Christ to be saying, Granddad thought. Then with great fervency and much theatrical demonstration, the preacher began to list the sins of the people until they shuddered in their seats at the awfulness of their thoughts and deeds. Granddad cringed down in his seat. The preacher stormed out the words of Christ. Dramatically, he thrust his hand to his eye as if to pluck his own out and Granddad thought for sure he heard the preacher's eyeball hit the floor. He caught his feet up for fear it might roll and stop right at his seat. Never, never had the Word been made so alive.

Granddad made his escape from the tent with a sigh of relief. The reality of the message haunted him long after his escape, but something compelled him to return for more abuse to his self-righteous Christianity.

Again Granddad sat trembling in his seat as the words of the evangelist hit his innermost thoughts and deeds. Still Granddad made his escape from the watchful eyes of the "brothers" who urged sinners like him to the mourner's bench.

And again, Granddad was back for the third night. This time he waited outside for a group of folks with whom he could slip into the tent to avoid the handshakes. He was sure they could see conviction written all over his face. His heart pounded so loudly it frightened him. He, J. A. Wilkerson, fearless of any man, was being shaken by the words of an evangelist—a holiness one at that!

The message was on the coming of Christ for the Church. In sonorous tones the evangelist rolled out warnings of hell, fire and brimstone. He took his audience to hell, back to earth and then on through the gates of heaven. Granddad got as far as hell. He thought he felt the fires of hell begin to lick about his feet. Soon his trousers had caught fire! The voice made a pleading call for sinners to come forward. Granddad half stood, gasping for air. "God, I'm one of those sinners," and he stumbled to the altar. In that instance, all the pride, all the stubbornness and all the arrogance of J. A. Wilkerson melted under the scrutinizing eye of the Holy Spirit. In that instant, the angels rejoiced, for a sinner had come home.

Granddad got up from that mourner's bench a new creature. He felt the newness—as if a ton weight had been lifted from him. The inner distress and guilt were replaced with peace.

Now Granddad always did things in a big way and getting religion wasn't going to change his demonstrative nature. He just couldn't turn and walk out of that tent without letting God and the entire congregation know how he felt. Not my grandfather!

Granddad forgot about his weakened condition, forgot about his stiff leg and really let loose. Suddenly, realizing the miracle that had been wrought, he let out a Yankee yell and took off. Around the tent he stormed in and out of benches, as if he were chasing the devil who had so long been chasing him.

Granddad was free and everyone knew it. Unashamedly, he felt the tears streaming down his face. Then remembeering his diseased body, he stopped to tell God: "Lord, you can take me any time now. I'm ready to die."

Up until that night Granddad had fought to live, trying any remedy suggested to him. Now that Granddad was ready to meet God, his only desire was to die. His tuberculosis had reached the last stages and there was no remedy of any kind left. The doctor advised him to set his house in order and wait to die.

However, Granddad wasn't about to permit thoughts of death to overshadow his wonderful experience. He never doubted for one minute his change of mind and heart, although his relatives and friends publicly voiced their skepticism. They knew Granddad had gone far from his upbringing, and they weren't too sure that getting so emotionally overwrought about taking a stand for Christ really proved that anything had happened to Granddad. You either did it or you didn't, and emotions weren't involved. And for a man to cry. . . ! It won't last, they predicted.

Only one person believed Granddad had changed and that was his wife. Grandmother had prepared in advance for the news of her husband's transformation. Within several days of receiving the message she arrived in Danville with Kenneth and Gertha. She had known the first thing her husband would want would be his wife and children.

I wish I could say Granddad's conversion brought about total happiness in their family reunion, but it was difficult for either of the parents to hide his sadness from the children. Different religious views had divided the family for a short while, but death meant separation forever.

Granddad went for his usual checkup and the medicine both he and the doctor knew had no effect either way. Granddad testified to the Doctor of his conversion; then, wistfully thinking, added: "You know, Doc I sure wish God had healed my sinful body as well as my soul. Some of those folks at the tent said He could, but I reckon that's asking God too much. At least I know now I'm ready to die."

Granddad left the office with that wish. The tent meetings were still going strong (revival fires were burning brightly), so Granddad shoved the bottles of medicine in his pocket and stopped by to enjoy some more of "that good preaching".

His spirit needed a lift and a visit to the tent gave him that needed inspiration. He even dared to believe that God could heal—and if He could, then why not J.A.? The evangelist made his plea for sinners to come forward and for the saints to gather round them. Granddad dropped his head, he was too weak to join the others at the altar.

A soft voice spoke. "Brother Wilkerson, this is God's night to heal you." Granddad lifted his head and, for a moment, only stared at the woman standing beside his bench; then, without hesitation he got up and obediently followed her to the altar. Folks gathered around him, some put their hands on his head, others on his shoulders and then, with arms raised up to heaven, they commanded in Jesus' name that Satan loose his hold upon J. A. Wilkerson's body.

When their prayers subsided, the good sister leaned over to Granddad and said, "Brother you're healed now!" Granddad hadn't felt a thing except the forcefulness and earnestness of the people's prayers. He got up, whispered a hoarse, "Thank you", and went home.

No one asked Granddad if he were healed. No one asked him to breath deeply three times. They prayed, they believed and then pronounced him healed. When he left, they thanked God for answering their prayers.

When Granddad got home he told his wife, "Honey, cook up a pot of beans and a batch of corn bread. I'm starving."

"Why, James, you know that will kill you."

"Not anymore, Della, I've been healed tonight." Then Grandmother heard the events of the evening. She not only complied with his request but added onions to the beans. She knew how much he loved them.

The first thing Granddad did the next morning was to head

straight for the doctor's office. "Doc, I've been healed. Now, no one's going to believe me, not even you, so I want you to X-ray me again so I'll have proof."

The doctor already suspected his TB patient possessed a great deal of determination, so he agreed to Granddad's request, wondering to himself how his patient would receive the news that nothing had happened. Needless to say, one look at the X rays was enough proof for the doctor that God still performed miracles.

Granddad didn't need those X rays to convince himself that God had healed him, but he planned to prove his recovery to the doubters of the authenticity of his testimony. Granddad declared skeptics set their minds against miracles and refused to believe—even if miracles happened before their eyes. He saw some swear by theories not backed up with facts and he planned to use his X rays as full proof of his healing. He was sure this would change the minds of the skeptics and pave the way for leading them to God's way of thinking.

By now Granddad could look back and see the hand of the Lord humbling him to a position of needing God, and he wanted to make up for his stubbornness by giving himself completely to God. Remembering his past and the insult that he had shouted to the heavens, he now prayed: "Lord, if you still want me, I'm ready."

3
Changing Pews

FOR THIRTY YEARS Granddad had walked in the counsel of the ungodly, stood in the way of sinners, and sat in the seat of the scornful. He figured his deeds were justified by the bold print of his name inscribed on the church rolls. Now, after a score and six years, Granddad was turned by the power of prayer toward the mirror of Truth and shocked into seeing the scoundrel that he was —proud, deceitful, arrogant and full of self-righteousness.

Then, in an instant and on two separate occasions, a miracle incomprehensible to the human mind was performed by God on J. A. Wilkerson. God did for Granddad what man had dreamed of doing for thousands of years: He provided a new heart, new lungs, a new stomach and a new leg, making a dying man live, with an extra promise of making his life eternal. Granddad had proof positive of the operation by the Master Physician—he was a condemned man still alive!

Something else happened to Granddad , too. Now it was God first, others second, and J.A. last. According to Grandmother, "That in itself is a miracle!" At last the Wilkersons were a real family. Little Gertha and Kenneth thought their "new" father the most wonderful man they'd ever met. He could tell them stories until they laughed themselves to sleep, and he would boost them on his back for the wildest galloping rides they'd ever had; but best of all were those little surprises—a bit of candy, a doll, a ball. Anything their father brought home was a delight.

With his hands busy working and his eye on the needs of his family, Granddad's mind was thinking of what he could do for God. He had committed himself to, "Anything you want me to do,

Lord." Granddad wasn't so foolish as to sit around waiting for God to tell him what to do—not after all that God had done for him.

My family's view about going out into all the world to preach the Gospel is very simple. We take Christ's words literally; "Lift up your eyes, and look on the fields; for they are white already to harvest" (John 4:35). My father never refused to preach when asked. In our family there were no prejudices in preaching the Gospel and the fields were all around us—our neighbors, our community or any who might inquire about the hope within. Our example for such an unbiased religion was Grandfather.

He looked out and beheld the wicked town of Westville with a population of about five hundred and took off in a horse and buggy to reap souls from its forty-five saloons. Granddad, with all his exhuberance, had a keen mind for details. Tell Granddad what you wanted to do and he could tell you in sixty seconds flat how to do it—successfully! He planned his strategy and set out for the attack.

Westville's drunks were too dazed and too busy huddling around pot belly stoves to keep warm in the bitter winter to notice strange goings on above one of their hangouts. Granddad and a friend cleaned out an old storeroom, installed a coal stove to heat it, enough hanging coal-oil lamps for their congregation to find its way with the least amount of stumbling, and then they stretched out wooden planks among a dozen or so "sanctified" beer kegs for the pews.

"Now," said Granddad, proudly viewing the crude chapel, "let's dedicate this upper room to God." Had the windows been open, the town would have heard two preachers storming the heavens to bring the wrath of God down upon their wicked city.

For a month, Granddad and his friend, Brother Bill, faithfully drove their old grey mare, kindling wood stacked under the buggy seat, to their harvest field. They lighted the stove and lamps, then warmed themselves on their knees in prayer. The homemade sign in the window said, EVERYONE WELCOME, but no one took the bait. Night after night Granddad's mandalin filled the room with the old-time religion songs. They prayed loud enough to be heard above the noise below them. They formed Jericho marches around the beer kegs claiming at least one soul within the sound of their voices. Then they stopped to listen: not a footstep was heard. Granddad's faith never faltered: "Just you wait, one of these nights we'll hear the footsteps of some sinner who needs God like I did,

39

and we're not going to let him out of here till he repents!"

When Granddad instituted a program, it never failed, because it was planned provisionally, subject to change the minute Granddad thought it needed revamping. "Brother Bill," Granddad announced to his friend one night, "it's time we put feet to our prayers." It meant cold feet, for the snow was piled high and no plows went before them to make the paths straight as they trudged from door to door, hoping for a warm welcome from just anyone at all.

It takes a stranger in a foreign land to recognize another in the same situation. So happy were Joe Debarber and his family to have two kindly and sober gentlemen drop by for a visit that they threw open their door inviting them to warm themselves at their kitchen stove.

Granddad sat down and leaned toward the stove to warm his numbed hands. Then he sat back with a big smile and proceeded to rattle off his glorious testimony. Eight pairs of dark eyes stared, their heads nodding. "Yah, yah," they responded, as if understanding Granddad's first venture at preaching.

Then came the clincher. Granddad meant business. "Now, Mr. Debarber, God wants to make you a new man. He wants to save you and all your family."

"Yah, yah," was all the poor man could say. He did not want to insult these nice men who could talk so well in the language he was trying hard to master.

Granddad could see he either had to learn Italian quickly or depend on God to get the message across. He tried his best to make the message plainer. Very distinctly he asked, "Will you let me pray for you?"

Ah, prayer they knew. Many, many times they prayed—to the saints, to Mary, to Jesus, to God. "Yah, yah, you pray for us."

So Granddad prayed as only he knew how. Oh, how Granddad did pray! So loud, so long, so fervently—for all the Debarbers. They stared in amazement. "Oh, oh, dis man, he wake Papa," whispered Mama Debarber.

Out came Grandpa Debarber in his nightshirt, spilling out words no doubt unrepeatable in any language. Granddad flashed another big smile, invited them to come to revival services and made haste to leave.

The next evening, Granddad and his faithful partner began the service as usual, their ears alert for the sounds of footsteps. Granddad felt something in his bones. Sure enough, soon there was the sound of heavy footsteps. Their hearts stopped pounding and they stared at the door. Very slowly it opened, and there stood Mr. Debarber looking apprehensively about the room.

Granddad and Brother Bill almost tripped over each other getting to the door. "Mr. Debarber, Mr. Debarber, welcome, welcome! Come . . .", then remembering the man's difficulty with their language, Granddad slowed down, "Come . . . sit . . . right . . . in . . . the . . . front."

For the benefit of their "audience", they started the service over. They sang, they prayed, and Granddad preached; only this time Granddad made his message as plain and simple as he knew how, being careful to conduct the entire service as though a hundred people were present. They didn't mind that their smiling parishioner was not able to participate in the songs or prayer, because of his language barrier, but it was of the utmost importance for Mr. Debarber to understand that he must come to the altar and make a profession of salvation.

Mr. Debarber understood clearly Brother Bill's request to "come . . . to . . . the altar . . . to . . . pray," but he could not fathom why they must pray with him. Granddad was getting anxious; he wasn't going to let their first "fish" out that door until he found Jesus as his Saviour. "Mr. Debarber, God . . . is . . . here. Can't . . . you . . . feel . . . Him . . . talking . . . to . . . you . . . telling . . . you . . . He . . . wants . . . to . . . come . . . into . . . your . . . heart?"

Mr. Debarber listened hard, watching Granddad mouth the words. "Yah", he nodded his head. He was understanding but, "I see no God." Patiently, hour after hour, Granddad and Brother Bill took turns trying to get the truth into the man's heart. At long last the light of truth dawned upon the soul and Mr. Debarber haltingly prayed the sinners prayer. Had it not been for the instant joy that filled the heart of their first convert, Granddad would have thought the repenter only admitted guilt to escape their clutches.

Further proof of Mr. Debarber's conversion came the next night when eight more people sat on the pews and listened with smiling faces as Granddad preached. Their congregation grew and grew, until finally they moved from the chapel into their own church.

By then Granddad had joined the Pentecostal Nazarene Church in which he had been saved. Because he had a hunger to know the

Scriptures and because Granddad wasn't one to appreciate anyone knowing more than he did he took the advice of his superiors and entered the Olivet University of the Nazarene Church. Being able to retain almost everything he heard or read, Granddad began a diligent campaign to memorize the Scriptures.

At the time he joined this denomination, the name Pentecostal was attached, but great controversy arose because of this Book-of-Acts experience occurring again in the twentieth century to people of all religions. When the Pentecostals joined together to organize a fellowship, the Nazarene church wanted the world to know they were no part of the fellowship and wanted nothing to do with speaking in unknown tongues. They voted to drop the name Pentecostal.

Granddad was young in his faith, but not young in years. He wasn't about to let any body of men decide for him what was *of God* and what wasn't. He searched the Scriptures and approached his teacher, Sister Serena Jay, with the thought that they certainly needed this experience to help convert the world. He couldn't see where Jesus limited the power to the Apostles.

Sister Jay was quick to warn Granddad to be careful. "Much fanaticism is sweeping the country: you must not get involved with this false doctrine. Forget about it and learn the deeper things of God, such as santification."

Granddad was a willing and earnest seeker of the truth. He regarded the words of his godly teacher with respect, temporarily putting this part of the Word from his mind, but thinking to himself, "Someday God will show me the meaning of this experience."

Being zealous and quick to learn made Granddad a good preacher, and he was no less cooperative with his brethern. Word spread about J. A. Wilkerson: "Let this man preach for you and the people will come running to the altars." It was so! Granddad had recalled the dramatic preaching that had swayed his heart. It was a simple matter for Granddad to combine his knowledge of Scripture with a theatrical flair—he had been born with a quick wit and a natural ability to hold the attention of audiences with his antics. He knew they would be accustomed to the expected, so he gave them the unexpected.

Once Granddad wanted to bring the congregation face to face with the awfulness of hell. He came across firecrackers that day in the local store, planked down a few cents and stuck five of the crackers in his back pocket. When he came to the part about the fire and brimstone in his sermon, he deftly pulled the firecrackers out, all the while preaching to hold the attention until they were lighted. *Ah's* and *oh's* from the congregation told Granddad the fire and brimstone he had dropped at his feet had taken effect. The altars were exceptionally crowded that night. The reality of hell had hit home to both sinners and saints!

Granddad was elected as the Chicago Central District Evangelist and served in this capacity for three years. One eventful evening during a tent revival he was holding near Olivet University, Granddad and his band of ministerial students came face to face with a group of Pentecostals who had come to hear this well-known evangelist. They came with their song books and Bibles tucked under their arms, their faces beaming with the glory of the Lord. The appearance of these "fanatics" casued a good deal of anxiety among the students. All during the song service they kept their heads bowed praying in a low murmur to rebuke the devils in their midst. Their agitation became all the more apparent when they noticed Granddad warming up to the visitors who sang with vigor and joined in the prayers as if they were right next to God.

One of the young men dared to step forward and warn the evangelist: "Don't let these devils get hold of our service. They're bound to scare the rest of the folks away."

So far Granddad hadn't seen any devils. The Pentecostals kept their seats just like any other church goers. "You let that be my worry, I know how to handle devils!" Calmly he listened to the testimonies, trying to ignore the angry sounds behind him. It didn't take long to discern which was the Spirit of Christ. After that service, not a person attended the revival. The tent had to be taken down and Granddad moved on.

Not long after this encounter Granddad felt he was meant to go back to his hometown of Knoxville. He especially wanted to give his testimony to his friends and to let his doctor see what God could do.

To become a traveling evangelist, Granddad was required to break up the happy family. Plans were made to put Gertha and Kenneth in the Wesleyan Methodist boarding school in Greenville, South Carolina. It was a hard decision and a sad one, but Granddad had put God first and he willingly made the sacrifice of parting with

43

his children, not realizing the affect of his decision upon them.

Granddad had a glorious ministry all through the South, beginning with the Patton Street Church and the Beaumont Wesleyan Methodist Church in Knoxville. The meetings often lasted four to six weeks, with people faithfully attending each night and bringing their unsaved friends and relatives. Grandmother worked right with Granddad, praying with the ladies and conducting afternoon prayer meetings.

The revival meetings were ofttimes met with vehement opposition. Granddad was noted for spelling out the sin question. He didn't care if the town depended on tobacco or corn to keep them prospering. He still stormed the platform, marching down through the aisles and shaking his fist at the devil, declaring that smokers and drinkers were defiling the temple of the Lord and that the wages of their sin was hell.

In Loudon, Tennessee, Granddad stirred up a real hornet's nest. He dared to preached right at the members of the Odd Fellows who were sitting in the congregation and gave away some of the lodge secrets which he felt were contrary to the Scriptures. The fury that shook the lodge members exploded into a plan to kill the evangelist. The local blacksmith gladly volunteered to do the job, vowing that he would not let that damnable preacher out of town alive. Word spread as fast as a brush fire from house to house.

Tension ran high that night. The church was packed. There were faces peering in every window and guns in every corner. The only calm one among them was Granddad! He got up to preach—a rustle of feet was heard—Granddad closed his eyes, about to ask God to bless the Word, when up jumped old Grandma Ruby. Down the aisle she headed, her eyes a-blazing. She faced the congregation: "This preacher knows God and I know Loudon. The first one who lays a hand on him will get *this*," and she pulled an eighteen-inch butcher knife from under her apron and held it high for all men to see.

She sat down in the front pew while Granddad preached a stirring message. It was by far the best night of the campaign. Many souls were saved, many bodies healed and the faith of the congregation rose to greater heights because of their victory over the enemy of their souls.

The Odd Fellows met to make new plans, but one of the members stood up and said, "Brothers, my wife's attending that meeting and

I'm not going to lay a hand on one soul up there." Another man stood and said, "My mother attends them services and I ain't a-gonna have nothing to do with this either." They could not come to an agreement as to how to get rid of the evangelist, so they adjourned.

Almost everywhere Granddad traveled he met with opposition from both the godly and the ungodly. Though Granddad had that charisma that held audiences spellbound, it was the effects of the power of God that brought people out to the services night after night for weeks at a time. No one could deny the power of God to change men and women from their wicked ways and no one could deny those who were healed. Granddad attracted people to his meetings by testifying about what the Lord had done for him. He walked through the streets, in and out of stores, saloons, and offices of town magistrates and pinned them down to attending church that very night. If they weren't there, they'd be sure to get that second invitation. If there still was no response and Granddad felt a burden, he'd get everyone praying until the sinner repented. If the rebellious one would not listen to his pleading, he'd say, "I'm shaking the dust off my feet. Hell will be ten times hotter for you now, my brother!"

Granddad spent two very successful years traveling in Tennessee and the surrounding states. At a meeting in Nashville, the course of the Wilkerson household was changed. Their children, Gertha and Kenneth, had spent many lonely months at the boarding school seeing their parents only on rare occasions.

Gertha was the older of the two and took it upon herself to mother her little brother. Still, little Kenneth cried his heart out every night, wanting so much to be with his mother. No one could console him. Bravely, they both endured school until finally Kenneth was worn out and listlessly gave up. "My brother's just homesick," Gertha told the doctor who examined him.

Gertha decided to end their tragedy once and for all. She took all the money she had saved up, left the school without a word and bought herself a train ticket to Nashville. Her mother and father stood dumbfounded when they saw their twelve-year-old daughter walk into the service. Her extreme measure worked! From then on the children were with their mother. This experience of my father and his sister was never forgotten. Dad vowed, "My family will never be separated from their parents."

J.A. rented a home in Knoxville and went out alone to preach. When World War I started, Granddad could no longer depend on his offerings to support his family. He applied for work in his old company, but they went on strike. Waiting out the weeks for a settlement, Granddad found himself involved in an unusual ministry because of the flu epidemic which eventually affected almost every family. Granddad traveled side by side with Dr. West, the physician who had once told him there was no hope for his recovery, on his rounds to the sick. "Dr. West fed them pills and I fed them Gos-pills," said Granddad.

Since no settlement of the strike seemed in view, Granddad decided to go to Ohio where the northern subsidiary of the traction company was hiring motormen. The family stayed behind until Granddad could save sufficient money to pay their fares to Ohio and also to purchase a home. It took one whole year, but once again, the Wilkerson family was united.

In the files of the Northern Ohio Traction Company are papers that tell of a strike settled by one of the workers who also was an evangelist. It seems Granddad wasn't going to sit down and take the strike of his company lightly. He had a family to support. He had worked with the men of the company for four years, he knew the cause of the strike and he knew a few hidden secrets of some of the bosses.

Granddad went into action with one of his "programs." Straight to the president he went: "Mr. Scanlon, I believe I can help settle this strike. Just give me a chance to preach to these men on Sunday afternoons in the barn and you'll see a miracle."

Mr. Scanlon was skeptical, but being a devout Catholic he hoped the spiritual influence might do some good, so he granted permission. Granddad entered the barn on the following Sunday, took off his shoes, jumped up on the large table called *the mahogany* and started preaching to the men who were gathered in small groups around the tables, gambling. One by one, men put down their cards. Some listened, some scoffed, but Granddad shouted above the complaints, telling it like it was. "Some of you men have stolen from this company, most of you cheat on the time and work you give the company, and yet you sit around expecting the company to give you better hours and better pay. What you really need is clean hearts and clean minds."

46

They heard about their drinking, their smoking, their women, their cheating. No sin was left that was not uncovered. "And furthermore," Granddad warned, "this strike will not be ended until you change your ways, pay back the money, promise to give a full day's work and start living for God. It's repent or starve."

A few Sundays of Granddad's old time religion began to hit the mark. When it came time for the next meeting of the leaders to settle on the contract, they gladly signed. The strike had ended. The president called Granddad into his office; "Mr. Wilkerson, this strike has been settled by your preaching. Now I want to know what I can do for you."

I guess Granddad could have had just about any position in the company at that time. Granddad had his mind on only one goal—to win more men to the Lord. His call came before himself and his family. "Mr. Scanlon, all I want is permission for the barn to be my church every Sunday."

Mr. Scanlon gladly obliged. Each Sunday the tables were moved aside, seats were set up and Granddad stood on the mahogany. Many men were converted and out of that group two made a decision to preach the Gospel.

At the same time, Granddad was having a new spiritual experience himself. He had met the preacher of a Pentecostal church in Akron by the name of Charles McKinney. This friendship lasted through their lifetimes and led to Granddad's finding out more about the "devilish" doctrine of the Pentecostals—that of speaking in an unknown tongue. When Granddad learned the experience would give him more power to preach the word, he made up his mind he was going to receive this baptism of the Holy Spirit. He didn't care if it *did* mean he'd speak some other language—that didn't seem so unusual to him. He was always learning, and gaining a new language sounded intellectual, not devilish.

Soon afterward Granddad received an invitation from his nephew in Alcoa, Tennessee, who pastored a Church of God congregation. It was in this revival Granddad experienced the power of the Holy Spirit coming upon him. It happened right in the middle of his sermon and Granddad thought for sure he was being translated right to heaven.

The first thing Granddad did when he got back to Akron was to find a Church of God. There happened to be a little chapel on

47

Massilon Road with a congregation praying for God to send along a pastor. The night Granddad dropped in for a visit, they had their pastor.

Then without warning, tragedy struck the family. Grandmother had seldom been sick. When she became ill, neither she nor Granddad felt her loss of strength to be alarming. "It's just this tooth that is bothering me," she said. But the tooth was much worse than they thought and it was too late to stop the blood poisoning in her body. Grandmother died on October 22, 1922. Granddad had accepted the position of district overseer along with the pastorate. He felt it impossible, with his busy schedule, to keep a large house going so he sold the house and furnishings and moved the family into a small apartment.

Grandmother had been the mainstay of the family: both the children were closer to her than to their father. Their grief was more deeply felt because Granddad was so busy with his duties.

In February, he received a call from the church in Fostoria. The pianist for the revival was a beautiful young woman who served the Lord with her musical talent. Granddad took one look at lovely Maxine and told the pastor, "I intend to marry that girl."

Granddad took unto himself his second wife on March 15. Their marriage was preformed in Toledo by Reverend Rembert, the state overseer of the Church of God. Granddad was no longer lonely and he was more than pleased to have a helpmate in the work of the Lord. He was of the opinion that all preachers of the Gospel needed a mate just to keep them sane!

To the two children who needed a mother and father to help them in their teen age lives, Granddad's marriage was a mighty blow. Gertha decided she would not wait any longer to marry the young man to whom she was engaged, but she worried about her brother. She had promised her mother she would always make sure her little brother was taken care of. It was Granddad who made the decision about seventeen-year-old Kenneth. There was no room in the two room apartment, so Kenneth (my father) was boarded out in the home of a parishioner. This sudden uprooting was a hard thing to take: Dad made his decision to part with his father and make his own way in life.

After his new marriage, Granddad kept his pastorate and position as district overseer for several years; then he received a call to be a pastor in the South. While there, he came into sharp disagreement with the policies of the church and decided to break with the Church of God and enter the fellowship of his good friend, Pastor McKinney.

His first pastorate with the Assemblies of God was in Hammond, Indiana. Granddad took a small congregation, put a strong spiritual program to work and built up the church to one of the denomination's finest. Just as in his revivals, he met with much opposition because of his unconventional ways, but Granddad had a way with people and they had to like him in spite of his antics. Many converts joined the church and many men and women went into the ministry from the Hammond church. In fact, I personally got to know two of them very well! So you see, Granddad must have had some faith to influence his own son and more than that—his daughter-in-law too!

4

And the Situation Is Well in Hand

At SEVENTEEN my father left his home without any thought of claiming the only kind of inheritance his father could give him. To a lonely teen-ager, the memory of a praying mother and the testimony of a father's healing were insignificant as an inheritance to take with him into an unbelieving and cold world.

Dad's first venture took him to Detroit to work on the assembly line in the Ford plant. Granddad saw to it that he was settled in a respectable boarding house and gave him stern advice to stay out of trouble, but Dad's inexperience in finding his way in the world resulted in trouble not many weeks after. Just what misdeed he committed, no one can tell me. It could not have been serious enough to warrant a brush with the law, but it did *brush* his father the wrong way. Granddad had to leave a revival meeting and travel to Detroit to settle the matter. A serious conference between father and son resulted in the conclusion that son Kenneth still needed some guidance. The best plan seemed to be to take advantage of one of Uncle Sam's opportunities for service to the country.

Dad chose the marines, and for him it was like stepping into another world. Immediately he found it satisfied all his needs for the particular time of his life. Besides a good place to sleep and the surety of three meals a day, he found the activities of shining brass, polishing shoes and being a world traveler kept him too busy to feel lonely. Adhering to the rigid rules gave him a sense of accomplishment and importance.

Dad entered into his new adventure with more zeal than a right-living minister's son should possess. Deliberately he chose the paths of sin that would completely disengage him from any connotation of holiness. Suddenly he was a man, and he intended to prove himself as much a man of the world as any other marine.

Fearing that his deceitfulness might find him out, he informed his buddies right off that he was the son of a Methodist minister. Since no reproach was attached to membership in such a well-known and respected church, he was allowed freedom to be just like one of the boys.

At times he overdid his role as a liberal and his marine buddies would shake their heads in amazement. "Wilkie, you aren't like we imagined preacher's sons to be." He drank, he smoked, and he gambled as if this were the only way to live. He was proud they'd never be ever to call him a *Holy Joe!*

His willful ways proved to be his downfall, though, and revealed him to his buddies for what he really was: a young fellow so packed full of holiness preaching that it had to come out sometime. It seems an unusual phenomenon occurred when Dad had a couple of drinks. By nature, Dad was serious and intense about life, but give him just two drinks and his personality was transformed from that of a sedate Methodist layman to a hell, fire and brimstone preacher.

It got so members of the ship's crew were disappointed if Wilkie wasn't along on their drinking sprees to give them their weekend sermon. They had become accustomed to hearing his deep southern drawl issue the command: "Okay fellows, y'all line up for a sermon. Y'all nothin but a crew of sinners in need of repenting."

Obligingly the marines, high on unholy spirits, staggered into some semblance of a line. "Preach it brother, we're all here and accounted for!" And with bleary-eyed intent they swayed to Dad's singsong sermon.

"Brethern, this drinking and gambling is nothin' but the devil's device to snare your soul. If y'all don't repent, I'm heah to tell you where yah spend the rest of yah life. Now tell me, my buddies, is it heaven or hell?"

"Heaven, brother, heaven." they chanted back to their spiritual buddy. And they called for more. They had never heard such preaching—certainly not from a Methodist! Dad would preach until he was talked out and that was mostly because he was sobering up.

Unfortunately, these preaching sprees could be manifested only under intoxicated conditions. Consequently his preaching had little effect on his spirited congregation. Yet the Bible does say that

51

God's word will never return void. Marines hoping to escape the Gospel message found themselves hearing it in the most unlikely place, under the most unlikely conditions. In spite of the manner in which it was delivered, it brought to their remembrance the truth they had been taught at home, and their consciences were troubled. Often fellows would approach Dad to know more of what he had been taught. Dad never minded sharing his religious heritage as long as a marine was sincere, but he was sure to tell them, "I'm only telling you what I heard my father tell."

Dad's satisfaction with service life made him a top-notch marine. His dependability caused him to make the right decisions at the right time and led to his capturing the more enticing jobs.

Just after boot training, orders to sail for Haiti were posted. Each marine was instructed to pack his duffle bag with a complete change of uniform. In their excitement to become world travelers most of the marines shoved their clothes into the bag, but Dad carefully placed polished shoes, socks, underwear and odds and ends in the bottom of his bag and then placed his well-pressed uniform on top.

When the order "Stand for inspection for the general," boomed over the ship's speaker in the port of Haiti, the marines hastily assembled on deck, wrinkled and disheveled. Only Dad and four others stood there tall and straight, dressed immaculately from head to toe.

"Marine, step out," the general ordered. Dad stepped out and saluted, and down the lines the general proceeded, issuing the same order to the other alert marines. They were told they were selected for the trusted position of shore patrol because of their neatness and generally good appearance.

Unknown to Dad, the general kept track of his chosen few and Dad soon received a greater honor, becoming an orderly to the general. This taught Dad a lesson on living by the rules which he never forgot.

His first hitch, spent mostly on duty in Haiti and the St. Thomas Islands, changed Dad from a bewildered, uninformed boy to a confident, well-trained and dependable young man. At the end of his four years, he felt he was ready at last to face the world; but when he found himself back in Akron right where he had started, he discovered his predicament not much different from four years earlier.

He was still without a home, although his sister and her husband readily opened *their* home to him. To make matters worse, in all his training Dad had never saved for a rainy day and now he was penniless. So there he sat, literally without one cent, unskilled and much too proud to borrow from his sister. There seemed to be no jobs available for former orderlies to generals. His stepmother's brother, Gillam, heard of Dad's dilemma and wrote a letter inviting Dad to Toledo where jobs were plentiful. Gillam never received an answer from my father and years later, when they became close friends, Gillam asked Dad why he had never replied. When Dad answered, "I was so broke, I didn't even have enough money to buy a stamp." Gillam asked no more questions.

It was natural Dad would look to the only life he knew for his career. Rejoining the marines for a second enlistment gave him a higher rank. Now as a sargent he was made a recruiting officer and stationed in Cleveland, Ohio.

Recruiting men for the marines wasn't as easy a task as shore patrol. Eight hours of the day he stood inside, or sometimes outside, a small booth located in Cleveland's public square. It was his job to encourage men to enlist in the marines rather than in the army or the navy and it called for some fancy talking. Dad had his mother's authoritative air and a generous dash of his father's gift of oratory. He and the other marines took turns sizing up a fellow. For the final inspection, one of them told a joke and, while the prospect let out with a hearty laugh, the other marine checked the candidates teeth. A good set of teeth was a must for the marines.

On his free time, Dad and his buddies frequented about every dance hall in Cleveland, in spite of their tired feet. Dad fared as well on the dance floor as he did on the job—especially one spring night in 1928.

Standing just inside a dance hall he searched the floor, sizing up the girls about like he did on the job, but with a different eye, of course. Spotting a lovely blond gal flitting around in the arms of another man, he boldly cut in, taking into his arms a girl perfectly described as "five-foot two, eyes of blue."

Before the evening was over he had laid claim to the blond, but Ann Martin wasn't so easily convinced as she was already engaged, and had been for two years. The only committment she'd make was where she worked. She had no intentions of falling for a perfect stranger.

The next morning Dad surprised the pretty secretary by meeting her as she got off the street car at the public square.

"Well, Seargent, you don't waste time, do you!"

Dad was about like his father. He never wasted time—not when he knew what he wanted. It did take him all of three months to convince Ann to marry him, though!

Mother married Dad for about the same reasons Grandmother had married my grandfather—except, of course, she thought Dad a good Methodist! Mother had been raised in a religious home; both her parents were good Lutherans who made sure their children studied catechism. Actually Mother knew her Bible better than Dad, but she never developed a close relationship with God such as Dad had been taught. Mother's prayers were limited to a few written ones she had either memorized or read from a prayer book.

She knew her parents would be delighted that she was marrying a Methodist minister's son. She couldn't wait to take him to Canonsburg to meet her parents and receive their blessing. Just as she had thought, the Martins were pleased their daughter had found such a fine gentleman, one with such a good religious background.

Mother and Dad began life together in a small apartment in Cleveland. They were very much in love and life was beautiful, except for one dispute which would never be resolved. Mother expected Dad to attend her church. Dad refused. "Then I'll attend the Methodist church with you," she insisted, wanting to start off their marriage in one accord. Much to her consternation, he even refused to attend his own church. A few arguments ensued, ofttimes taking place around the table of their friends living in the apartment below them.

"I don't want to attend your church, Ann!" Mother couldn't understand what was so wrong with the Lutherans.

"And just what is wrong with my church?"

"Well, if you want to know—your church is dead!"

Mother laughed. She was inclined to agree, but she knew no other church. "Well, my dear husband, at least you can't say we act like the Holy Rollers." She wasn't sure how they did act, but she had heard they danced and shouted, even going so far as to roll on the floors.

Dad pushed back his chair, his eyes blazing: "What do you mean by that remark, Ann? Are you calling me a Holy Roller?"

"Why, Kenneth, why are you so angry? Why should I call you a Holy Roller? I don't even know what they are; anyway, you can't say Methodists are Holy Rollers!" Mother simply could not understand her husband's strong reaction.

Dad checked his anger; a confession was at the tip of his tongue —it had been since the day he married. Now he could never reveal that his religion was often called The Holy Roller Church. Mother eyed Dad with suspicion. There was a reason for his anger she was sure; someday she would learn the truth.

Dad kept putting off the day of wrath and, fortunately for him, he wasn't even around when mother solved the mystery of Dad's angry outburst.

They had been married only a few months when orders were given for the Cleveland recruiting office to close up and send its men to report for duty at Quantico, Virginia. Mother was expecting their first child and since Dad did not want to leave her alone while he was settling in a new post, they accepted Granddad's offer for her to live in Hammond where he was pastoring.

Dad had married without asking permission of the marines. Granddad advised him to set things straight and ask to be relieved of duty to take up a career more suitable for raising a family. Permission to marry was denied, so Dad decided to try the truth —*still* they refused to relieve him from duty.

"Son, you go on to Virginia. My church will pray—God will get your life set in order!" Mother and he parted; Dad went back to the marines and Mother went to Hammond to live in the parsonage.

Mother was made welcome in Hammond, but she sensed something just not quite right. She had put her best foot forward, carefully attiring herself in her most modest clothes (which weren't very modest, according to holiness traditions). She even toned down her makeup. On the weekend, she dutifully announced she would attend their church services.

Sunday morning they drove up to a large barn-like building; at first glance Mother was sure it was not a Methodist church, but on immediate inspection, the inside appeared no different from any other sanctuary. She was pleasantly surprised to see such a large crowd—that spoke well for her father-in-law. Then, as newcomers are naturally prone to do, Mother began looking about. Several strange peculiarities were quite evident. She realized at once she was *not* modestly dressed. Her makeup—even the style of her hair was all wrong. Of all the weird happenings! People, during the prayer, had their arms raised up and all prayed together! Some were even speaking in foreign languages.

"Why, these people are crazy!" she thought to herself. Then the light dawned. Kenneth *was* the son of a Holy Roller preacher and she, a staunch Lutheran, was sitting in a holiness service! "How will I ever get out of this?" She would have to think of some way.

Granddad knew what the reaction of his new daughter-in-law would be. With great wisdom he let Mother figure out for herself what she must do with her discovery. They made her feel at home, all the while going about the Lord's business as they were accustomed and never once explaining or apologizing for their peculiar behavior.

Mother left the service that morning declaring to herself that she would never go back again and get mixed up with such a group of oddities. Unknown to Mother, Granddad had already taken the request for Ann's enlightment to the ladies' prayer meeting. Son Kenneth was included in those prayers. Now it was "Operation Children" in the Hammond church.

Granddad did let Mother know they were praying for Kenneth to be released from the service. Mother believed in prayer and she graciously thanked her in-laws, but she was more pleased about the prospects of her husband coming to take her out of the holy surroundings.

It seemed to Mother that the Wilkerson family lived more at church than at home. Prayer meetings and Bible studies filled each morning, afternoons were spent visiting parishioners and at night were the evangelistic rallies. For awhile Mother viewed the routine with disdain. Gradually she accepted her in-laws as they were, and slowly but surely the prayers of the women began to have effect. Like spring slowly blossoming forth, Mother's interest to know more about God grew. Emerging from her self-righteous shell, she made her second announcement: "I'm going to your church this Sunday." Curiosity had gotten the best of her. She had to go back once more.

This time the people didn't appear to be crazy. This time the spirit of the meeting reached deep inside, plucking a chord of longing held so long within. During the spontaneous congregational worship, my proud, Lutheran mother raised her hands toward heaven and for the first time in her life she audibly gave forth heart-felt worship to God. And it felt so good! It was like a new birth of her soul. At last she had her first real religious experience and what it did for Mother lasted her a lifetime.

For the first time she found Christianity a joyous and satisfying faith. She wanted to tell everyone she met what God had done for her, and especially she wanted her husband to know. "Honey," she wrote, "I've been really, truly saved." Dad couldn't believe it. What had they done to get his stubborn wife to see her need for a deeper meaning than her staid, formal Christianity? He would have to see it to believe it.

Now Operation Children spotlighted on Dad. To his amazement, orders for his release were granted. Almost before he knew it, he was on the train speeding through several states to Indiana. The clicking of the wheels penetrated his troubled conscience. Suddenly he heard himself say what the clicking wheels seem to say to him: "I'm going to get saved, I'm going to get saved," was repeated over and over with increasing intensity.

The message stayed with Dad. He arrived home, giving no hint of his decision to accept the faith of his father and now of his wife. It wasn't until Dad attended church and boldly stepped forward for salvation that the entire church knew their prayers had been answered. That very night Granddad added step two to his plan of Operation Children. He intended to see that his son was thoroughly grounded in the Scriptures. He meant to give his son what he had so neglected during his son's teen-age years.

5
Back to School

MY FATHER'S exposure to a variety of training programs seemed to be processing him for one profession—the ministry. Dad told us that there were times throughout his growing-up when he knew for sure he would someday enter the ministry, but he put it from his mind feeling very unqualified to offer himself for such an awesome work for God.

Granddad had no qualms about my father's future. He felt sure his son, with his help, could follow in his footsteps. With exactly that theory, Granddad launched Dad into a study of the Word and of his own unique philosophy on pastoral theology. Each day Dad got up he shadowed his father through ministerial duties: sometimes Granddad had him pray, or encourage a parishioner on their visitation rounds, or give his testimony to strangers whom Granddad might stop on the street, and occasionally Granddad yielded his pulpit to Dad for a short sermon.

Mother watched Dad's growing process for several weeks with mounting annoyance, until one day she spoke her mind. "Kenneth, we can't keep living off your father. There's not enough room for us here, either. I think we should get our own place, and have a steady income." Mother was concerned for that steady income as much as having a place of their own. She hadn't been accustomed to being without. Her job had provided an abundance of clothes and money for doing whatever she pleased. Entering into a life of poverty didn't set too well with her and that seemed exactly where they were heading if Dad didn't soon find a good, paying job.

Dad, by this time, had gotten totally involved in the activities of the church and it took every bit of his time. This is how he liked it, it was like meat and drink to him, but earthly duties called. He had no intention of being a burden to his father or letting his own family suffer, so without a word to anyone, he began the search for a job. He arrived home one day tired but happy: "Ann, I've got a job! And you'll never guess how much I'll make—forty dollars a week! Imagine that!"

Mother was overjoyed. Now they could move into their own apartment, buy furniture and, best of all, replenish the wardrobe that had suffered under Dad's nonprofit training program. To add to her joy baby Juanita arrived. It seemed she had every thing to make her happy. She was even finding a deep satisfaction in Dad's Holy Roller church.

Spiritually, Mother felt she was making great strides. As a Lutheran, Mother had learned Bible history and had memorized many of Christ's teachings, but her church had never taught her to apply the Scriptures to her life. Now she was sitting under Granddad's teaching and applied Christianity is where Granddad excelled.

Mother couldn't seem to learn enough. Willingly she accepted all she saw and all she was taught. Day by day she found her worldly ways not in keeping with Granddad's standards of holiness. Since Mother had a sincere desire to achieve true holiness, she felt she must follow explicitly the teachings of her father-in-law. If Granddad said it was wrong to wear feathers in hats, she believed him. When he preached against jewelery, mother eyed her wedding rings with feelings of guilt. The more Granddad preached against it, and the more she saw others putting rings, watches, and other accessories on the altar, the more the rings bothered her. At last she could stand them on her finger no longer. Without a word to Dad, she sent them back to Cleveland, shocking not only Dad, but the jeweler, too. As for the holiness hair styles, she resigned herself to wait patiently for Mother Nature to see that her short, bobbed hair grew to a godly length. Only then could she pull her hair straight back into a modest bun.

After a few months of Granddad's indoctrination, Mother was definitely not the same worldly Ann who had arrived attired as a Jezebel, and her change found favor with her relatives and with the church members. Mother's greatest change took place in her own home: she obeyed the Bible's admonition to find a secret closet of prayer and to study to show herself approved. Unknown to Mother, she was being prepared for a job she would never have bargained for, but one that was going to require all the self-discipline she now gained.

There were times in Mother's life when she faltered over Granddad's strict holiness, but in those early days of her Christian growth, Mother established a love and faith that sustained us all—and still does.

All the while Mother was going through her own growing program, Dad was working eight hours a day, rushing home for supper and then off to church to assist his father in anything he might be called upon to do. On the weekends, street meetings were conducted right in the heart of Hammond's shopping area. Like Granddad, my father had a built-in sound system and he could carry a tune on key, so Granddad put him in charge of music and testimonies. On very rare occasions Dad could expand his testimony into a sermonette.

Gradually Dad's Christian walk showed maturity and after a few months he approached his father about trying out his preaching wings. Granddad lined up a few speaking engagements in several small churches with the instructions: "Now, son, know what you're going to say, back it up with Scripture and give it to them with both barrels."

That's the way Granddad did it, and he thrust his newborn preacher out, expecting his message to soar to fervent heights, moving the souls of those who listened to mountain top experiences.

To Dad's utter dismay, he found that he wasn't ready to fly. His sermon descended with a thud; but Dad made one important discovery on his first solo flight in the pulpit—he was *not* the shadow of his father. Oh, he had inherited a few characteristics of Granddad. He had that charisma: he could hold his audiences spellbound to the Word, but he couldn't exhibit in Granddad's style. Any attempts to be like his father ended in disaster. He lacked an ingredient and he knew it. What it was he could not guess, but without it, he knew every sermon was doomed to failure.

Granddad issued an ultimatum: "Son, you just aren't ready to go out on your own. You need more training, and more than even I can give you." Then he told his son the vision God had given him. "I saw a barge loaded with fruits and vegetables in the middle of a riverbed, but there wasn't a drop of water and the barge couldn't move. Son, I believe God has a great ministry for you, but you are like that barge, you lack the water of the Holy Spirit to get it moving."

Dad held his father in high esteem even though he couldn't follow along with some of Granddad's ways. He felt if his father had received a message from the Lord that it came as direct guidance for him and he must heed the warning.

Dad taught us children that God not only makes plans for our lives, He carries them out. And if we would sit still and wait for the hand of God to move on our behalf, we'd receive guidance without any effort other than submitting ourselves to God's plan for our lives. Dad had learned this truth the hard way.

He continued to work and make himself useful in the church, all the while praying for God to show him what he should do. Several weeks after Granddad's vision, Dr. Miller of Peniel Bible School in Dayton, Ohio came to Hammond church to conduct a series of Bible studies. Of course, Dr. Miller heard about son Kenneth and his need for Bible training. The good Doctor listened and watched. He sensed potential in Dad and approached him with an offer that changed the course of Dad's life. "Kenneth, if you'll come to my school, I'll personally get you a scholarship that will take care of all your expenses."

Dad was positive it was God's answer to his prayer. His father said, "Son, this is God's way of answering your need." My mother said, "How can you go off and leave us here, expecting your father to support us—especially with our second baby coming?"

With his father so sure and his wife in tears, son Kenneth stood at the crossroad of a decision that would shape forever the destiny of his entire family.

I wonder, could it be that a mother's prayers were still effective? It must be so. Dad made his decision: "Honey, I feel the call of God. You must understand this, I am not forsaking you and the baby. If you're going to be a minister's wife, you must learn to trust God. Something will work out."

Words of promise were not enough for Mother, "I can't understand why God would separate us. Why would He join us together, then suddenly take us apart? I don't believe God works this way." Mother stubbornly stuck to her logic.

Fortunately, Mother had been quick to learn one of the strongest Pentecostal teachings—the prayer of faith. She went both to her closet and to the ladies' prayer group. "Sisters," she pleaded her cause, "you must help me pray. If Kenneth goes to school then I must go too." The sympathic women took to their knees; they were going to pray until help came through from heaven for Sister Ann.

August came, and school would open in less than three weeks. Plans had to be made for storing furniture and Dad had to give notice that he would be quitting his job. Mother and Dad made preparations for the move—Mother and Juanita to Granddad's, and Dad to Dayton. The departure day loomed like a day of disaster and still no answer to Mother's dilemma. Goodbyes were said and Dad left without his family.

Just two weeks later, Mother attended an all-day rally in Chicago with a delegation of women from the Hammond church. During the activities of the day, she met Mrs. Flem Van Meter, wife of the state superintendent of the Assemblies of God. The gracious lady gave Mother a warm Christian welcome to her husband's district and, before she knew what it was all about, Mother was sobbing out her story. "Tell it to a woman and it will get done"—this must be true. The power of the prayers of those church sisters brought Mother to the very person who could help. Mother isn't sure what went on between Mr. and Mrs. Van Meter, but soon after the services in Chicago, she received a call from the Bible school.

The call came from the school's registrar, but for Mother it was a message from heaven: "Would you like to take an office position here at the school? We understand you would like to join your husband. This job would more than meet your expenses." Mother didn't even bother breathing a quick prayer for guidance; she had waited for this moment for five weeks. In less than a week Mother and Juanita were together with Dad, living in one room of the dormitory.

Happily the family of three involved themselves in the life of the school. Juanita, then only fourteen months, became the school's mascot. She was passed from room to room and Mother had willing baby-sitters almost around the clock. By midterm she was toddling from room to room collecting pencils, pennies, candy or anything else her hands could grasp. Mother was able to keep up her secretarial duties, attend several Bible classes, keep house in their small room and carry their second child all at the same time.

Dad arrived at the school expecting it to be very much like the marines, precise and orderly, with everyone working toward one common goal. When he saw his roommate nattily dressed and hiding cigarettes in his suitcase, he had doubts as to whether school was what he needed after all. Watching the moonstruck lovers romance among the campus trees, he wanted to tell them the ministry was too important to be wasting time looking for mates. He felt God would see to that desire if they'd put first things first. He had already forgotten his marine's eye searching hundreds of dance floors for the perfect girl.

In class the students annoyed him to exasperation when they quibbled about trivial matters. He wanted to shout: "Grow up! Let's talk about the real issues. It doesn't matter where Cain got his wife."

Dad was older than the majority of the students and his service career had acquainted him with the raw realities of life. Though he had no difficulty adapting himself to studying, he could hold no toleration for the young, innocent and inexperienced scatterbrains he had to attend class with. For a long time these students were Dad's thorn in the flesh.

Weeks of exposure to annointed teaching of the Word stirred up conviction about his attitude toward his classmates in Dad's heart. He faced up to his unloving spirit and asked God for a measure of tolerance and love. His prayers brought forth the patience he needed and helped him to understand the needs of those younger than he. All his life Dad was a source of help and inspiration to the young folks in his churches and especially to young ministers.

Dad could spend only one year in school, but such a firm foundation was laid that he was able to build a mighty ministry upon it. To this one year, he added Bible courses from correspondence schools and hours of his own research through the Scriptures.

When school ended in May, Dad, and Mother and baby arrived in the Hammond parsonage just in time to take part in a conspiracy to hide three of Granddad's children (who were sprinkled with red dots) from the eye of the doctor who was attending Maxine with her fourth child. In the midst of their nursing, Mother had to be hustled off to bed—baby number two was due any time.

Granddad always managed to involve himself deeply in the affairs of the church at such delicate moments and Dad, though willing, had too little experience to successfully run a miniature hospital, so Granddad exonerated himself by hiring two nurses— one for duty downstairs with the measles patients and one with the mothers on the second floor.

Maxine had a baby girl and christened her Mary Ann, and mother had a ten-pound baby boy and named him David, praying that truly her son would be another David, killing many giants for the Lord. David was the only one of us who could brag that he attended Bible school even before he was named. Dad supplied the second name, Ray, in honor of his marine buddy who had taken Dad home with him when Dad had nowhere else to go.

While Dad was seeing to the affairs to this family, Granddad was mapping out his son's future. The nearby community of Indiana Harbor lacked a Pentecostal church and Granddad took it upon himself to see that a mission was established in this town of steel mills. What better prospective pastor could he choose than his own son?

Dad eagerly joined in the plans, his enthusiasm overriding momentary feelings of apprehension. His father's assistance and the wholehearted cooperation of the church soothed the moments of doubts. How could he fail backed up by such staunch support!

The Hammond church put time and money behind their pastor's effort, securing a small groundfloor hall with a three-room apartment in the back. Of course, there were a few disgruntled parishioners especially other young men who had a call, who opposed the pastor's son getting the choice arrangement. As usual, when Granddad set out to do anything, he did it in spite of opposition.

Dad and the volunteers worked hard. They went from house to house inviting people to the new church. They gathered together each night, holding services and hoping to attract the passers-by. When one method failed, either Granddad or Dad came up with another, but it seemed this venture had been doomed from the very beginning. The town just wasn't interested no matter what they had to offer. Dad marked the episode *failure* in his mind and gave his thoughts to charting another course.

This failure really shook Dad's confidence. He felt he had failed his father, the church, his family and worse yet, failed God. Talking, thinking and planning only confused him. In the midst of his turmoil, Dad suddenly realized he had never really asked for divine guidance in his efforts to establish a mission. His father had paved the way, help was available, and it had seemed the thing to do. He had seen no reason to question the validity of the mission.

I would say it was during this moment of perplexity that my father began a new venture—one that took place on the knees, physically transporting him absolutely nowhere, but spiritually transporting him to what we mortals call sainthood.

Dad did some asking—"Lord, what shall I do?" Because Dad had no pride before the Lord, he confessed his need for God's guidance. Then he waited. Dad told us it was the waiting that caused folks to give up their dependence on God. Asking is easy; the waiting is difficult.

Happily for the family, Dad wasn't kept waiting. A member of Granddad's church opened up his home to Mother and Dad while his wife was away for a three-month visit to her family. All they needed "to pray in" were three meals a day. They knew from experience how to do that, but when you pray in *your own* food, you don't have to be so particular. Praying in food for the landlord and host takes more and finer prayers, but they did it, and Brother Brown never knew but what they had a substantial income for he was eating pretty well.

In those days, though, the big issue wasn't food. Dad need a place to preach. "Where, Lord? Open up the door, Lord." On his knees in their bedroom, Dad beseeched God for some direction. The trousers of his only suit showed signs of inevitable catastrophe around the knees, and still they waited. . . and waited. But the heavens seemed as brass.

About this time, Mother had just about had her fill of "waiting on the Lord." She took her husband to task: "Kenneth, I think you've waited long enough. It seems to me God doesn't expect us to sit around defeated. It's time for you to get out and find where God wants you."

Mother's anger stirred Dad up. Now he approached God with determination. "God, I've got to know why you haven't led me to do something or go somewhere. I can't move without your direction or I'll make the same mistake. You've promised to direct me and I need that direction NOW." Dad felt a rise of his spirit, but whether from anger or from praying the prayer of faith he wasn't sure, until he started to get up and his line of vision fell on an old car across the street in Brother Abbott's backyard. His backbone stiffened. What right did Abbott have to own *two* cars when he didn't have even *one*—and needed one to get out and preach the Gospel! He got up and, with faith, strode out of the house and across the street to Brother Abbott's front door.

Faithful Brother Abbott never dreamed his old car could be

commandeered to preach the Gospel. It was all right with him if Kenneth needed it, but he warned: "It sure could stand some fixing up. The battery is gone, the tires are worn down, and it could use a new paint job. Haven't used it in years." Once Dad set his mind to a venture there was no difficulty he couldn't surmount, especially when he received direct leading from the Lord. He told the church folks of his need and the people caught the spirit of the venture. Donations came from dozens of people and soon the car was in tip-top shape—for an old car, that is.

Mother viewed this new approach for finding a pastorate with more than a few qualms, but if it brought results she'd be satisfied. Another young man who had a call to preach and had attended Bible school with Dad—and who also needed a church—offered his services in overhauling the car, providing he could go along to find himself a church, too.

Herman and Dad began traveling-by-faith on Saturday morning, heading their car south on Route 41. They arrived late in the afternoon at Attica, a good-sized town in western Indiana. It was a Saturday-night town. Farmers were in town to shop and the streets were full of people strolling from store to store or just standing on the corners exchanging the latest gossip. Dad looked at the milling crowd and said to Herman: "Herman, we're going to have a street meeting here!"

"How? Who ever heard of two men holding a street meeting without singers, or anyone to testify." Herman was a downright skeptic.

Dad answered, "Watch me." He dropped to the sidewalk on his knees and with a voice that could raise the dead, he started to pray with his arms stretched heavenward. When he finished he had his crowd. First, Dad preached; then Herman preached, and when they had preached themselves dry, they closed the meeting and stood watching the crowd slowly disperse wondering to themselves, now what? Neither of them knew what they'd do next. Before they voiced their suggestions as to what to do, a listener approached them with the solution.

"If you brethren have the time, our little mission is without a pastor, and we need someone to preach in tonight's service. If you have the time, it would be nice to have you preach for us."

Herman looked at Dad, and Dad looked at Herman: "Did they ever have the time?" their eyes flashed the same thought. They not

66

only had time to preach a second sermon of the evening, but they also took time to respond enthusiatically to an invitation to remain overnight for the Sunday services. Dad was asked to preach again at the mission and Herman was directed to a nearby church that also needed a pastor. After the evening service, a quick conference took place between the deacons and the members and they decided to hold an election right then and there before Dad could be on his way. Dad was unanimously chosen as pastor of the Attica Pentecostal Mission on the first ballot, and Herman came from his church rejoicing with similar results.

Dad and Herman took off in a burst of glory for Hammond, like Elizah taking off for heaven, except Dad's chariot sped along on a puff of smoke rather than on a ball of fire. They sang, repreached their fine points to each other, they shouted, and they laughed— and they wondered why preachers had a hard time finding churches. In the blaze of glory, Dad's past failure faded; he could hardly wait to tell his wife and father. How happy they'd be to hear of his instant success! Dad sighed with satisfaction and whispered a heartfelt prayer of thanks as they entered Hammond. Now at long last, he was Pastor Kenneth Wilkerson. It had to be God, of that he was sure.

6
Lord, What Now?

THE FIRST YEAR of pastoring was a time of initial fulfillment for Dad. To be preaching and pastoring a people was enough. For the first time they felt they were home. The parsonage, though small and without adequate kitchen facilities, had a spacious yard for the two children to play in. The congregation demonstrated their appreciation with offerings of vegetables. The only drawback appeared to be the location of the church on a third floor.

Dad's zeal for the ministry grew and as it did his vision to do something worthwhile for God preyed on his mind. Dad was never one to be satisfied with the status quo and he was quick to tell this to his congregations. First, he prepared them with faith-building sermons and when he felt they were ready, he charged forward presenting a new program for the church. In this case, Attica was badly in need of a new building.

Life had glided along without a murmur until Dad began preaching about launching out. In each sermon he thrust a challenge before them: "Folks, we sing, 'Launch out into the deep, cut away the shoreline,' but what you really mean is, Lord, don't let it be too deep, it might cost me something."

It always amazes me that congregations balk, sometimes with more stubbornness than a mule, when a pastor wants to lead them into greener pastures. In every church Dad led through a building program he had to endure the wrath of a few unbelieving saints and often those righteous mules were board members.

The first hint that trouble was brewing came from a man who had become a member of the church before Dad's arrival, without making a true confession of faith. Now, under Dad's anointed preaching, which ofttimes pointed out the sins of the people, the man showed his true colors. In order to mislead the members and keep them from discovering the real villian, the wayward saint began what Dad referred to as a whispering campaign. The campaigner's goal was very evident—he must get rid of the pastor or be shown up for what he really was. It isn't very hard to make a pastor look bad—there are so many to help point out his faults.

Dad took these crises as personal affronts from Satan to the church. Since he had no intention of being defeated by one already defeated by Christ, Dad would boldly announce to the congregation: "Beloved, I will NOT allow Satan to rear his ugly head in our midst." With righteous anger, a-kin to that shown by Christ as he turned over the tables in the temple, Dad would preach right *at* the one being used by Satan. On this occasion, Dad chose an even finer technique for separating the sheep from the goats: "I want all those on the Lord's side to stand by the altar on my right, and all those on the devil's side stand to the left." The entire congregation, with the exception of the guilty member and his son, stood at the right. Even the man's wife refused to stand against the pastor.

That night in the home of the wayward saint, his wife had a dream. In tears she woke her husband and told him she had seen him heading toward a precipice and he had fallen, screaming for help. Dreams and visions were very much a part of the Pentecostal faith in those days and the tragic scene struck fear into the heart of the husband. Early in the morning, he rushed to the parsonage. When Dad opened the door, the man literally fell in the door begging forgiveness of him and of God for his sinning. Dad prayed with him a prayer of deliverance against Satan and from that day on the man became Dad's righthand man. And Dad needed one.

All the while the people fussed, fumed, argued and complained, Dad went ahead with plans to build. Positive that he was doing the will of God, Dad determined to reach the "promiseland" even if no one followed. God honored his perseverance and brought along a Christian contractor who offered his services without charge. While the church building went up, the congregation dwindled down, and down with them went the finances, the gifts of food, and the general goodwill of the people. Now their situation was reversed: no money, no food, no members. In the midst of these adversities, son number two arrived. He was named after Dad, *Kenneth*, but we called him Jerry.

At last the church was ready, but by now Dad was exhausted by the people's attitude and the joy of accomplishment had already ebbed. Hoping that a revival service might revive the congregation, Dad called his friend, Gillam, who had entered the evangelistic ministry, to hold a week's meeting.

Gillam well remembers that first day of revival: "Your father opened up the service and right off began denouncing the people, ending his short sermon by resigning from the church. Then he turned to me and said, 'Let's get out of here.' Hardly knowing what had happened, I strode out right behind him and my poor wife, completely bewildered, followed behind me while the audience sat dumbfounded."

Dad had reached his limitation of tolerance. Now he was no longer Pastor Wilkerson. Fortunately, before beginning the building program, Dad had rented his own home nearer to the church, so at least they could not be forced from their home. But without money they could not eat, could not pay for a car Dad had recently purchased, and couldn't pay the rent. "Lord, what now?" It seemed to Dad he was always praying this prayer. Now that he had acted so hastily, it would be hard to choose the safest path.

Dad and Gillam talked over the situation. They both needed either a charge or churches in which to conduct revivals. There was only one choice—track them down. Mother and Cliffa, Gillam's wife, and the children were to stay behind. The Ohio District Council would soon be in session so plans were made to travel toward that, seeking meetings in towns along the way.

Off they started to points unknown. Gillam can laugh now remembering those harrowing days. "As we were cruising along at the lightning speed of thirty miles an hour, we suddenly saw a sign: PENTECOSTAL TABERNACLE. Right out in the country! We stopped, of course. Inquiry revealed that a trustee lived in the vicinity. We looked him up and introduced ourselves. He invited us to stay and preach the next day, Sunday. Now you can imagine our reaction when we learned we had stopped at a *Free* Pentecostal church. (*Free* was a sure sign they took too much freedom in the Lord.) Kenneth said: "We'll give them the straight Word. If they never hear it again, at least this time they'll get the truth." So we gave it to them. First, I preached and in twenty minutes I was preached out; then Kenneth got up and opened both barrels. They didn't know what to do. They sat as though stupified. He tried to

70

make an altar call but they sat. He exhorted them again, and still they sat. Finally, he gave up and turned the meeting over to the leader. Well, the meeting sparked right up. They began to sing and then someone got up and began to dance; then more followed right out in the middle of the aisle. We sat while they shouted and danced. After a while they quieted down and the leader reached for his hat and coat. Then, as if it were an after thought, he announced they would take an offering for the visiting ministers to help them on their way. Kenneth and I were surprised but very much delighted. We thought that here was the answer to getting to the council, but when we counted the offering, we decided to abandon our venture and hurry back to Attica."

Again it was, "Lord, what now?" Dad was discovering hasty actions often are followed by indecisive choices. Again Gillam and Dad pondered their situation. They both still needed a place to go. Well, first off, Dad decided, the car he had recently purchased must go back to the dealer, and certainly they couldn't go back to Hammond admitting another defeat. No ray of hope seemed to break through the clouds of doom. Gillam had a car, so they packed all the furniture in one room, loaded the car with clothes and kids and headed toward Cannonsburg, Pennsylvania, to the home of Mother's good Lutheran parents.

My grandmother is a kind, generous person. With open arms she welcomed her daughter's family and their friends, although Grandfather Martin couldn't figure out how two ordained ministers could be without charges. Mother's sister, Helen, who had visited them while they lived in Hammond and had been converted under Grandfather Wilkerson's ministry, felt their sudden appearance a direct leading from the Lord. Her newfound zeal for serving the Lord gave her a burden for her own hometown and now she desired to see a Pentecostal work there.

For months Helen had been saving money for just such a time. Now she was prepared to help all she could. While Mother and Helen searched the town for an apartment, Dad made a tour of the downtown area for a hall they might rent, and Gillam offered to go back to Attica for their furniture, using a four-wheel trailer he had stored at the home of his parents in Toledo.

Mother's house hunting ended on top of a high hill and on a third floor. Dad found a hall in the heart of town on the ground level. The failures of the past dimmed as they moved toward a new challenge.

Dad warned us about the ways of Satan. "Just when things begin to go good, keep a lookout for Satan. He's not far behind, ready to put a wrench in the works." Dad spoke to us from experience, for he was no sooner settled in the apartment than Satan attacked the entire family with a physical disease. They knew only that it was called *the seven-year-itch*, although actually it never lasted that long. Unknowingly, they had carried the tormenting itch all the way from Ohio. Now, Mother, Dad, Juanita, Dave and Jerry were in a sad state of affairs, scratching, and the children were crying with the misery of their suffering. The only remedy offered was the application of a concoction of lard and some unknown ingredient to all part of their bodies. For three days and nights they lived in grease. As was the custom of my father, he approached God about their predicament, but before he could utter a word, Satan taunted: "Look at the mess you're in. God's punishing you for your failures. He doesn't care about you and your family. Why don't you curse God!"

That was all Dad needed to hear. His righteous indignation rose up. In the name of Jesus he rebuked the adversary and claimed victory for his household. His bout with Satan ended the itch. Victory had come through prayer. Now they were ready to forge ahead in the Lord's work.

Gillam returned loaded down with their furniture. Mother and Dad, just over their seige of illness, were happy to see Gillam and Cliffa, but there wasn't enough food in the house to prepare a meal, with the exception of what had been sent from a relative in a gift package that very day. Overjoyed to be receiving a box, Mother had torn off the brown wrappings to discover a few odds and ends of clothing for the children and, in an old raincoat, were four apples. How they wished every stitch of clothing had been a box or can of food! What could two hungry families do with four apples?

Mother came to the rescue. "I do have a little flour and just a speck of shortening left. Maybe I could make a pie."

"A pie!" They thought Mother had taken leave of her senses. Whoever heard of eating dessert before eating a meal? But Mother can be very determined at times. With the bit of flour, shortening and four apples she produced an apple pie, using a bread box for an oven on top of the stove's open flame. Proudly, she reached in for her lucious, browned pie. She doesn't know how it happened, but next there lay her prize, face down on the floor, smashed to a glubby mess.

They stared in disbelief. This was their only food. Cliffa is very practical. "Ann, the floor's clean." (Mother had just scrubbed it that morning) "Let's scoop it up and eat it." They all tell me it tasted delicious.

With the help of Helen's money and Gillam's ability, they readied the hall for services. Gillam used his carpentering skills and built a platform and pulpit. For fifteen dollars they purchased a piano, and even the town burgess offered help by securing opera seats for the hall. In a matter of a few days they were in "business."

They began nightly services with Dad and Gillam preaching alternately. By the end of the week, a few people made up the congregation. One night, the group showed considerable increase. Dad led the singing and then took an offering. From where Gillam sat on the platform, he saw a strange bit of action transpire between one member of the congregation and the offering plate. The man dropped in several bills, then suddenly, as if relenting his generosity, thrust his hand back in and *took out* several of the bills. The offering wasn't as good as Dad wanted for his guest speaker, none-the-less, it more than sufficed for Gillam to return to Ohio, so he figured out what he needed for gas and gave the rest of the money to Dad.

The next day they bid farewell and it wasn't until Gillam was well on his way that he remembered he hadn't figured on the toll bridge across the Ohio River. "What could I do, but turn back. I felt like a fool asking Kenneth for my money back. Of course Kenneth made some joke about it all."

In spite of the show of progress, Dad felt the Canonsburg effort was another exercise in futility. If it hadn't been for Helen, and Mother's parents, they surely would have starved. "Not really," Mother is quick to tell me. "God would have provided food through someone else." But there were days when stomachs groaned for lack of being filled. In vain, Dad sought a job.

Did he dare approach God *again* for help. Dad did; he *always* did. Dad believed God loved him no matter how weak his faith. A church in Findlay, Ohio, wrote asking if he could hold a revival series for them. Since the Canonsburg mission had been at a standstill for several months, Dad took this invitation as a sign God wanted him to move on.

Again it meant separation. No church would welcome an evangelist with his wife and three children. This time they stored their
furniture in Grandfather Martin's garage and Mother and the children remained behind, waiting for news that Dad had found
another charge.

Dad left for Findlay on the bus. After Findlay, he had no idea
what would be next. They could only trust God that some where
there was a house and a church they could call home.

7

At Last a Home

THE FIRST real home for us was in Barnesboro, Pennsylvania, but before we enjoyed those happy days, Mother and Dad endured two more trials of faith. From the revival services in Findlay, Dad went to another small church to conduct a week's revival. The church had been without a pastor for several weeks, so Dad's arrival couldn't have been timed more perfectly—for the church, that is. His one week campaign didn't bring the expected revival, not in Dad's estimation, but the congregation so enjoyed his fiery preaching that they asked him to remain as their pastor. Against his better judgement, he accepted.

This particular church (which I shall not mention by name since the efforts of several pastors have no doubt led the people into a truer way of worship), possessed what Dad called a "whoppin' and a hollerin'" religion. It was their version of a Pentecostal experience, and my father couldn't tolerate a put-on move of the Holy Spirit. He pounded away at their phoney antics with few results.

Mother had her troubles in this church too. Juanita was five years old, David three, and Jerry had just turned one, and all three of them showed signs of irritability from being shifted from pillar to post. Now in the cold and crowded apartment, they were turning out to be the rascals the church folks predicted they must be.

The second floor apartment, which served temporarily as the parsonage, was in the home of one of the parishioners, who evidently had never been taught about the fruits of the Spirit. Grudgingly she loaned Mother enough dishes for five people with the explicit stipulation that they be returned. "They were my mother's, you know." Mother could easily see that for herself. Impending

75

doom was unavoidable. Those cracked and chipped dishes seemed to be screaming for destruction. Mother did her best to handle them with care, but with three little ones, what could be expected? The culprit was David. He committed the crime of breaking a handle off one of the "priceless" cups.

You would have thought David had burned the house down, there were such goings-on by the dear sister. A sound spanking was soon forgotten by mischievous David, but Mother, always careful not to offend one of the parishioners, suffered the wrath of the sister who haughtily refused to accept Mother's sincere apology. Had Mother been able to offer to pay for the cup, the sister's wrath might have been abated. Poor Mother! She couldn't even promise to cover the cost of *one cup*—at least not while her husband pastored the dear sister's church. She had no money to make amends, and the little money Dad received on Sundays barely stretched to cover the cost of their food for half of the week.

But someone had money. There was the Lord, coming to their rescue again for such an earthly thing as a broken cup! Friend Gillam, who worked at secular jobs in between conducting revivals *happened* to be visiting Dad in the midst of Mother's crisis. Gillam had rescued them in many ways, but this was the first time he had to settle a feud between pastor's wife and parishioner. A few cents of his money solved their differences.

In Dad's haste to get out from under such pressures which were placed upon the entire family by members of the congregation, he moved to a church in Bellefontaine. The previous flock had at least presented a slim ray of hope, providing they called a pastor who was a bachelor and could exist on the few dollars the board felt sufficient for ministers living "by faith." Now Dad had jumped from the frying pan smack into the fire without realizing the situation—until Mother took a good look at what the board called the parsonage. When they arrived she found it already occupied with what David and Jerry thought were little puppies. It took several days and plenty of traps to rid the house of rats. The ticks and roaches took longer to get rid of—and far more grace to live with.

While Mother braved the indoor hazards, Dad braved the weather to walk several miles to work on a farm where he received a dollar's worth of produce a day for wages. It seemed an answer to prayer that enough vegetables could be earned to keep them from starving.

One day the heavens shook with thunder and poured rain down upon a dejected preacher of the Gospel as he wearily hoed the weeds. Suddenly a flash of lightning broke across the sky knocking Dad to the ground. He lay there with his heart pounding, foolishly wondering if he were still alive. Yes, he was alive, only something inside had died; the jolt from the sky had struck the deadness within waking him up to see himself as God saw him.

Here he was, a child of God, fighting the elements and the rodents—fighting to stay alive—when he should be fighting Satan and doing a victorious work for God. The lightning seem to strike his will to fight. The church at Bellefontaine might have given up the Christian fight long ago, but my father hadn't. Possibly it was too late for *their* bolt from heaven, but it stirred Dad up to seek a place where he was needed.

Churches weren't so readily available as he had once thought. Granddad Wilkerson had recently moved to Mansfield, Ohio, and Dad wrote asking if he knew of any churches open in that area. Granddad could only suggest churches that would be as difficult as Bellefontaine, but he did negotiate for a small Ford coupe so that Dad could go out and search for a charge.

The Depression had made its mark on churches. The small congregations could not afford to support a pastor—not one with three children—and pastors of larger churches knew better than to move during such times.

Christmas was nearing and the very thought of spending holidays in a cold house with no money to buy food, let alone gifts or a tree, was more than even the most saintly should endure. Mansfield wasn't too far away and it was a place to go. Dad almost felt like the prodigal son, saying, "I will arise and go to my father's house."

There was no royal welcome for one who had been gone three years and still hadn't found his place in the ministry. His father had begun to regard his son as a perennial misfit in the ministry. Dad's arrival with his family at this most inopportune season, bearing only tales of woe, didn't improve a father-son relationship. Granddad, involved with raising an entirely new family, found the presence of the old family, whom he thought had long since been launched, to be disturbing.

Dad was in no mood to withstand his father's grievance with him. Then, when he glanced at the packages under the Christmas tree and saw there were no gifts for them, not even for the children, it wakened past memories of his father thrusting him out on his own. He turned to Mother and said, "Get the children in the car." Mother obediently hustled Juanita, Dave and Jerry into the car without questioning. The visit hadn't lasted more than an hour.

As they turned on to the highway, Mother dared to ask her seething husband: "Where are we going, Kenneth?"

"To your mother's," were his only words. They drove to Cannonsburg in silence. Dad was too hurt to talk. The pain of his whole life swept before him. The hurt had been building up for a long time, almost all his life, and now it finally closed the door on any kind of close relationship with his father. He made up his mind that he would never darken the door of his father's house again.

They arrived in Canonsburg tired, discouraged and very hungry. Grandma Martin had no idea they had left their church; she was just happy another of her children had come home for Christmas. Grandma always prepared for the holiday season days in advance. There were all sorts of good things to eat and Grandma, with her "seventh sense," thought her daughter might show up and had a gift for each one of them. Money squeezed into Mother's hand during the day bought a few toys for the children who knew what it was to have a visit from Santa.

Mother, happy to be home, easily put the recent trials from her mind, but Dad could only sit and brood over his rejection by his father. He felt that even the Lord had rejected him. Mistake seemed to follow mistake. Was there no end to his woes? he wondered.

We sing a hymn in our churches: "Take Your Burdens To the Lord and Leave Them There." In his sermons, Dad would illustrate the way some of God's children took their burdens to the Father. "We approach Him so heavily burdened our backs are bent under the load." Then Dad would walk across the platform as if bent with burdens and kneel making a request to God that He take care of the problems. Then Dad would get up and go back to the pulpit, still bent with his imaginary load. Dad was sure his parishioners did this because he had done it too—way back during the depression years.

The Martin's thought their son-in-law quite a moody and unsociable kind of fellow. It was impossible for Dad to join in the merriment. Too much was at stake. Affairs between Kenneth Wilkerson and his God had to be settled once and for all, so off to the bedroom Dad went to "pray through." He had struggled long enough with his problem, almost forgetting God had a standing offer for His children to cast their cares upon Him.

I can only imagine what Dad told the Lord. I'm sure he admitted the error of his haste, confessing that he had brought on their present tribulations by his own impatience. Now he sought God's forgiveness, asking for a renewing of his weary spirit. It must have been then that he forgave his father, for Dad never showed he held a grudge, although he determined he would never again look to his father for any kind of assistance. He knew it was time he began trusting only his heavenly Father and walking according to His instructions.

How well I recall Dad telling me, "Remember this Ruth, God always loves you. He'll never reject a plea for help from one of His children." This was the greatest sustaining truth Dad ever taught me. I'm sure Dad had discovered this on his knees when crying tears of anguish and defeat and it had sustained him in the weakest moments of his faith.

During the unsettled days of the new year, God began to unfold His love for His children. Miraculously, He led them step by step until they were exactly where He planned them to be.

Soon after the holidays, Dad began his search for another charge, *this* time asking for God's guidance. He wasn't acquainted with the officials of the Pentecostal (Assemblies of God) churches in Pennsylvania so he did not know who to approach for assistance in locating a charge. One day as he read the denomination's publication, *The Evangel,* a very unorthodox idea popped into his mind. The magazine listed churches announcing coming revival services and Dad suddenly felt he should attend one of those churches. Which church? He did not know. As long as he was going out on the limb with his extraordinary thought, he saw no reason for not going all the way.

As if not trusting this simple act of human foolishness to be God's way of guiding, he brought Mother into the plan and asked her to pick the church. Since no great wisdom had been imparted to Mother, she did what any trusting woman would do. She closed her eyes, breathed a quick prayer for God to guide her finger, and then, without looking, she circled her hand above the page bringing her finger down to rest on the name of a town they had never heard of: Pitcairn. A map revealed it was a small town located near Pittsburgh, approximately forty miles from Canonsburg. Nevertheless, both Mother and Dad determined that was the exact church they must visit.

Leaving the children with their Grandparents, they set out very early on a cold winter Sunday. They found the church in time to attend the morning worship service. The congregation was small so the appearance of strangers didn't go unnoticed. The pastor welcomed them personally, of course, it led to the discovery that Dad was a minister of the Pentecostal faith, so immedaitely the congregation had a guest speaker for the morning.

After the service the folks thanked Dad for the good sermon. Some stayed to chat about where they were from and where they pastored. Hearing Dad was in need of a church, one of the members spoke up with a suggestion: I heard there was a church in the next section needing a pastor. You might try there, the town is Barnesboro, but I can't say for sure that they still need a pastor."

Dad thanked the gentleman, Brother Morgan, for this information and, after shaking hands with everyone he and Mother went out the door to go home. Unknown to either the pastor or the members, Mother and Dad had made the forty-mile trip on faith, with barely enough money to get there and none for going back to Cannonsburg. Dad expected to be called on to preach—that was the way of Pentecostal churches—and always an offering of some sort was given to the visiting speaker. Now they were walking away, their pockets empty, without one person even suggesting they be given an offering.

Just as they started to get into the car, the pastor came running down the church steps calling for them to wait. "Here, brother, the folks want you to have this." It was a five dollar bill.

Mother and Dad anxiously waited out the week. When Saturday arrived, snow was falling hard and the wind blew fiercely, but they had set their minds on going to church in Barnesboro on Sunday and all the words of warning from relatives went unheeded. Barnesboro was even farther than Pitcairn. They arrived late in the afternoon, made a few inquiries and at last found themselves at the home of one of the parishioners.

"Yes, we certainly have been praying for a pastor," the words of Sister Anderson were a soothing balm. Dad wouldn't let himself become too jubilant even though their gracious hostess seemed overjoyed they had come along. This time he was in search of a flock of sheep—not of mules and goats—desiring a shepherd to guide them.

Sunday morning, Dad stood behind the pulpit for his first service with not more than a handful of people. But by the end of the service he knew he had come across a fold of sheep and he wanted to be that shepherd who would lead them into greener pastures.

Dad believed in walking in the Spirit—this meant he expected to receive direct guidance from the Lord. He had come to realize by his hasty actions he had closed his mind to the Spirit's promptings. His prayer of forgiveness for such actions had renewed his spirit and again united his spirit in fellowship with God's Spirit. He could sit back and almost see the hand of God moving on his behalf. It set his spirit soaring to even greater heights of joy and thanksgiving than ever before.

When Dad felt this assurance of the Spirits leading he never hesitated to step out by faith to do something for the Kingdom of God; nor did he fear revealing his faith publicly to his congregation, or to whomever might be involved in his venture.

After the benediction for the evening service, Dad asked the congregation to be seated. "Folks, I believe God has sent us to you. You are without a pastor and I am without a church. I believe God has directed me here to be your pastor." *Amens* could be heard simultaneously from the small group and they did not think it strange when Dad boldly requested: "Those who want me to pastor, please stand." To ask for a negative reply was unnecessary—the entire group immediately stood on its feet." Dad had at last found the place where he was truly needed.

Because he was needed, he had no desire to prolong his arrival even though the church was without a parsonage. The congregation had no sooner approved Dad as a pastor when he made his second request. He had never before asked a congregation for anything for himself or for the family, but somehow he felt these people cared where the pastor lived so he asked that he personally might locate an adequate apartment or house.

That's how Mother and he happened upon a second-floor apartment in the home of two unmarried sisters who were too proud to attend a Pentecostal church, but who sympathized deeply with a minister who had three children, was expecting a fourth and had no place to live. Had they known Dad, by faith, would claim the entire house of seven rooms for his family, the Thurston sisters might not have welcomed our lively brood so wholeheartedly into their home. When that day came, only the neighbors thought it strange that the sisters would rent their home completely furnished and then go right next door and rent an apartment for themselves.

I was born in that house on Philadelphia Avenue just a couple of months after my family's arrival. My memories of living on that wide avenue are limited, but I do recall two stores, one on each of the corners across the street, that were hangouts for my two brothers. One was a candy store and the other a bakery. Orders were given that I wasn't to wheel my tricycle across the street, yet no one seemed to care that I was wasting my life waiting for either David or Jerry to emerge from one of the stores with a morsel of sweetness for me. I never did get my share of the calories.

Early pictures show both the boys to be pleasantly plump. There's no doubt the store proprietors could take credit for the preacher's sons being so robust.

One memory is outstanding to us all even to this day. Granddad paid us a visit and he didn't come alone. He brought three carloads —all his family and a group of young people from the church. It seems Granddad had a contest and the winners were treated to a trip. The victor's day came and about twenty people packed themselves and baskets of food into the cars and started for Barnesboro. I don't know if Granddad was rewarding his youth or wanting to show off how well his son had done for himself.

At night they joined our congregation in a service. As always, it was Granddad's day. He completely overwhelmed us all with his joyous, outgoing personality. Dad happily stepped aside and let Granddad take control; he knew his father had a way of getting people to respond to the power of God. Granddad took out his tamborine and really let loose, making a joyful noise unto the Lord. Then he taught us a new chorus:

> Oil in my vessel and oil in my lamp,
> Washed in the blood and sealed with a stamp,
> Jesus may come before another day,
> Oil is all I need.

We sang it again and again, and in between he told the saints they must make sure they had enough oil to get them to heaven. We children weren't quite sure what Granddad meant, so we sang out with great gusto hoping that would give us the oil. For many a year the Barnesboro congregation remembered the first visit J. A. Wilkerson made to their church.

Juanita (we now called her Nan because I couldn't pronounce Mother's choice of this exotic name), Dave, Jerry and I watched the day's proceedings in awe. It was our first real contact with Granddad and his family and we could see they were something special. "Boy, you should meet my Granddad," Dave bragged the next day in school. "He's better than any circus man—he can play and sing and preach and do stuff with his leg." Dave was completely enraptured by his unusual grandfather; his mind was set to dreaming of being a great preacher like his granddad, but he wasn't sure he could swing his leg right over a pulpit! Granddad added this demonstration to his sermons on healing (if it were a one-night visit to a church he did it even if his sermon wasn't about healing) to shock his congregations to the reality that miracles still happened. Granddad's legs were mighty long compared to Dave's, so David wasn't sure he'd be able to put on that particular demonstration.

Granddad could only stay one day but he was satisfied that his son had found his place in the ministry. Dad had become the shepherd he desired to be. He had begun his ministry in Barnesboro with just a handful of people who worshiped in a building they called a Tabernacle, but which looked more like a large barn in need of repairs. However, they were the sheep Dad thought they were, and faithfully they followed the shepherd who loved them. At the end of the first year, Dad wrote to his friend Gillam:

I certainly do appreciate my past experiences. They have enabled me to be an instrument in God's hands here. Our dear Lord has more than made up to us for the lean years. I can hoe out the weeds now and water the plants and have the pleasure of seeing them grow. Seeing the Word take effect is a great blessing to me. God has been good to the church . . . added twenty-five adults to our church roll . . . conducted a good business meeting—one in which the Spirit of Christ was present—and we were unanimously elected for another year. God alone knows what the year will bring forth—but He will be with us *come what may."*

8

Come What May

THERE ARE three of us who have followed the path of our father
—David, Don and I, and we look back to our Barnesboro days as
the time the foundation of our faith was laid.

The peaceful little community nestled in the Pennsylvania hills
was a perfect setting for a lively growing family. When we lived
there it was a mining town, but the mines were far enough away so
that Barnesboro never became the typical mining town America
has been blighted with in past years.

Living with a come what may attitude was a glorious venture into
a promised land for both the congregation and our family. Dad led
the people from one victory to another and they willingly followed
their shepherd. As the church prospered so did the pastor and his
family.

Dad's income increased so greatly from those of the lean years
that the household budget could finally allow one of his boyhood
dreams to come true. It seemed very long ago that he had vowed
he would purchase a home for his children. Now it was coming to
pass—and to Dad, the house was God's crowning blessing.

It was an eventful and exciting day when Dad returned the keys
to the Thurston sisters for a house the church had rented for four
years. Now we were heading toward the north end of Barnesboro
to our very own home, the *first* for our family.

Mother and Dad had searched the town for a house large enough
to accommodate four children and another soon to arrive. They
were so thrilled with the price and location of a large frame house
on a quiet street, they didn't seem to notice several uninviting
factors: the house needed to be painted and repaired, the front yard

looked like a desert, and the backyard a filthy and run-down barnyard.

A sure sign our church had the Spirit of Christ was the reaction to Dad's announcement that he had purchased his own home. No one minded that the pastor prospered abundantly. In fact, they saw to it that his salary swelled to include new furniture, money to make repairs and even a shining new black car came along as an added blessing. Then, like good Samaritans, the church folks went beyond the call of duty and pitched in as if *they* owned the house. Women brought brooms and pails and set the house in order. Brother Spike Wilson and young Danny Smith rolled up their sleeves and told Dad, "We've come to help, Pastor, where do we start?" Then Mother's brother, Albert, paid a visit and, even though he couldn't see eye to eye with his sister's religion, he couldn't resist doing a good deed.

In short order, our new home became transformed into a mansion. At least that is what it was to Mother and Dad after having lived in rat- tick- and roach-infested apartments. A more fitting parsonage couldn't have been chosen. Like magic they changed the barnyard to a park. Chicken coops were torn down, the land cleared and grass planted, and even a cement walk laid. David and Jerry struggled with pails of water and wheelbarrows full of sand and rocks while the men tried their luck at cementing a straight walk down the length of the backyard. The result was a masterpiece with not one crack and we children happily christened the job with our bicycles. Mother snapped a picture of the three jacks-of-all-trades and their two helpers for our "Hall of Fame."

This walkway divided the two-hundred-foot yard and on either side of the walk stood identical fruit trees at various intervals. First came two unpredictable peach trees, then a shady spot for the lawn chairs; next came our favorites, two large apple trees that also served as acrobatic facilities; then came Mother's victory garden and across from that a brand new set of swings with all the attachments. Several yards beyond our playground ran a shallow stream. Though the water wasn't deep, the walls were about four feet high so the men lined the sides with rocks and built a bridge strong enough to hold thirty men. It was a beautiful stream beckoning us to cool our tired feet, but Dad gave us strict orders not to go into that water. For a long time we couldn't understand his command —four inches of water certainly couldn't be dangerous.

The boys solved the mystery. "Do you know what's in that water?" David, the voice of authority, let us in on the secret. "It's from the outhouses." There were still one or two homes on the block making use of the outhouses, so we could only sit dangling our feet from the bridge looking longingly at the rippling water. To be sure, not once did we venture in.

In the yard at the front of the house stood a thirty-foot well that proved a satisfying substitute for the loss of a wading stream. It didn't take long to discover that throwing water at one another could be as much fun as wading. The well had existed for years and people came from all over the neighborhood and miles around for a taste of the cool, sparkling water.

We hadn't lived there very long when Mother and Dad realized that ofttimes the parched visitors were miners coming home from a Saturday night out on the town. They had had their thirst quenched at the local bars, and by the time they staggered to the house with the well, they felt desperately in need of a cooling drink of water. A wooden fence remedied the problem somewhat, except for the parched who could locate the latch and still had the ability to open the gate. Mother feared one of them might get more than a cool drink, so finally Dad had to close in the well.

When the major work was done on the outside of the house, the attic project began. This became a must on the day Dad opened the door of the middle bedroom and shouted down the steps, "It's a boy!" Everyone of us had been born in a parsonage and Don was no exception; he did have the privilege of being born in our own home though. I guess that's why he turned out to be so good-natured. At his birth, I thought everyone showed him a bit too much attention. It was hard to relinquish my favored position after reigning four years as the baby of the family. I must carry a hang-up after all these years because I still refer to my well-known and well-traveled six-foot-one brother as my little brother. However, jealousy soon faded when the three boys moved to the finished attic and I moved into my very own room.

Wisely, my father made only necessary repairs and additions to the house; both Mother and he had learned the importance of being frugal in a parsonage. (In those days, Dad's salary was on a love-offering basis, and woe to the pastor's income if he upset the cheer-ful givers!) But in the heart of everyone—no matter how fervently one desires to be holy—there must lie a seed of extravagance. My father could not resist the purchase of a handsome combination radio and phonograph. To add to his splurge he bought a dozen albums of semi-classical records that we played during our evening meals. Dad's love for music no doubt influenced his enjoyment of so worldly a possession. Fortunately, it had no evil effect whatsoever. In fact, we all rather enjoyed the music and it inspired Mother to see that we all took piano lessons from none other than one of the Thurston sisters.

Mother's extravaganza really took on only one of us—Nan. She seemed to have that same love for music as Dad. My desire to be a world-known concert pianist faded into oblivion completely under the spell of books, and Jerry's cultural experience didn't last even through his first music session. After Miss Thurston introduced him to his first piano book and instructed Jerry how to hold his hands over the keys, he simply said, "I don't want to," and walked out the door. To our anxious inquiries as to how he liked his first lesson, he nonchalantly replied, "Okay." It wasn't until David's turn that we found out the truth. I'm sure David longed to follow suit. He hated anything he thought sissified, but he would never admit defeat. He agonized through several lessons before getting the idea that saxaphone lessons were more manly; then the rest of us had to endure the weird sounds drifting out of the attic windows. The greatest protest came from our dog who sat in the driveway howling all through the practice.

Music was the only art we were permitted to develop and that only because our parents felt this knowledge would be useful to us if we entered the ministry. Our upbringing was definitely religious. Our entire lives were spiritually oriented until the day we chose to go out on our own.

Even before Dad met Mother, he knew exactly how he would raise his family. The large, comfortable home with its places for us to create joyous childhood memories were all a part of Dad's dream. Though we each remember that home with pleasant thoughts, it was the home Mother and Dad created through their training and prayers that still influences our lives.

God was the center of our parent's lives and they both adhered to Apostle Paul's instructions for the saints to do everything for the glory of God. The early Pentecostal concept of this truth meant an adherence to a very strict way of life. Dad's teachings of holiness closely followed that of his father; and Mother, never having been taught any kind of holiness except Granddad's, trained us in the only way she knew.

My younger brother, Don, and I lived through the Barnesboro days unaware of the many restrictions attached to our religion. Bicycles, swings, trees and hills were satisfactory worldly pleasures for us. David and Jerry lived a Tom Sawyer and Huckleberry Finn sort of life—though somewhat modified because of the strict training and Dad's method of taking care of overly mischievous boys.

It was the first born, Nan, who bore the brunt of the outward holiness standard that made her wonder why religion could make one so happy and yet so sad at the same time.

Nan loved scholastics and studied hard to make the honor roll. One day she came home bursting with pride, hoping Mother and Dad would be pleased to hear what the high-school principal had told her. "Mother, there's going to be a special program at school and the principal is going to present me with an award pin. Please, can't you and Daddy come?"

Mother and Dad were proud of Nan's accomplishments, but without hesitation Mother told her, "Honey, I'm sorry, but we can't go. Your father is speaking at a special service in a nearby church." Nan stood alone to receive her award for excellent grades, the joy of the occasion completely erased because no one was there to share the recognition.

My parents had nothing against education; their attitude of not getting involved with school activities had been influenced by the forerunners of our faith who looked upon education as one of the culprits causing the church to grow cold and formal. Public schooling was viewed as a necessary evil and college as an unnecessary evil. My parents zest for learning made them realize the folly of such a view; by the time Nan was graduated they could see the value of a college education.

More than any of us, Nan bore the pain of our Pentecostal faith travailing for a true Christianity. To her request: "Why can't I wear anklets like the other girls in my class?" she was told, "Proper Christian girls keep their legs covered." Nan endured the humiliation of standing out like a clown for only a short while—then solved the problem by sneaking a pair of anklets to school and changing. For her, the many *don'ts* usually dispelled the feelings of happiness and satisfaction the rest of us received from our way of life.

Of course, each one of us experienced some momentary disappointments. How well I recall the circus coming to town and all the neighborhood children bubbling with excitement. The animals I could manage to see by getting as close to the circus grounds as I dared, but I never ceased to wonder just what *did* go on in those many little tents. Daringly, I strained my neck as I passed the local theater to see what wickedness man could think of that would condemn him to hell. And on Halloween I prayed fervently that my parents wouldn't find out that the teacher had "forced" me to put my coat on backward and wear the false face she had cut out from construction paper so I wouldn't feel out of place at the school party. These shattering-but-for-the-moment happenings soon lost their devastating affect when I got home and entered my own kind of world.

Amazingly, with all its restriction, our religion brought much happiness. Our pleasures were found in the warm and sincere fellowship we had with God and with one another. As children, we felt secure in the faith of our parents—we were happy just knowing we were loved by God and by our family. As long as we unquestioningly lived the faith taught us, we lived in the security of knowing our lives pleased God. We were taught the importance of this, since true happiness can be found only in serving God. Our feelings of guilt and confusion came when we became teen-agers and began to rebel against the strict holiness teachings. Then all five of us struggled with the faith of our fathers, and each one of us had to find out for himself what *was* the Truth, the Life, and the Way.

Those growing-up years we spent in Barnesboro became a dependable plumbline, helping us to determine how to build on to the foundation of faith that Mother and Dad so diligently had placed before us. We look back now and know that we experienced the realities of life that God intended for man, and we were shielded from the realities that are the result of man's sin because our parents loved us. They had seen both sides of life and knew the better. Their restrictions were for our protection, but does a child ever understand this? Or was this a protection prohibiting us from facing reality? More than one preacher's kid, or Pentecostal layman's child, have proven that the strictness was a harmful protection, but understanding can bridge the obstacles. Our generation has learned from the mistakes of our parents; we know from our own experiences it is better they see both sides of life and are taught why and how to choose the better, but we can only hope and pray, as did our parents, that our way is what is best for our children.

We all readily admit we sometimes got hung up on our background; yet we must confess to ourselves that there certainly was never a dull moment around our parsonage. Too many eventful and happy times fill our memories—there's no need for us to dwell on the don'ts.

I never recall being bored. Why, even church was fun! To this day, I can close my eyes and almost see and hear those services we attended as children, and their warmth still lingers with me. I can see my father as he joyously led the people in making a "joyful noise unto the Lord."

Worshiping God through music held great importance in my father's churches, though not as much as the Word or prayer. Dad, a master song leader, made singing such a delight that often our services began and ended with a song service. Seldom would he permit anyone to lead the congregation in singing. "That's when I take the spiritual temperature of the people," he would say. If they dragged the tempo, or sang disheartenly, he would stop and say: "All right folks, let's come to church. Ladies, forget about the supper dishes, and, men, forget what time you must get up for work. Let's worship God." That challenged the congregation to sing their best. When we ran out of hymns to express our feelings toward God for his wondrous love, then we sang choruses. If a particular chorus touched souls, we would sing that chorus over and over, clapping out expression of our love to God.

During the singing of the choruses, Dad opened up this part of our worship for testimonies. Audience participation, which is woven throughout the services in various forms, brought much vitality to our services. No saint can refrain from sharing God's blessings: a thought may burn within, a prayer may have been answered, or God may have led a person directly to do a work for Him. During these "spiritual therapy" sessions, members could stand and testify or request their chorus. The combination of the two always resulted in stirring the faith of the people.

We children enjoyed this part of the service because Dad allowed us to request our favorite songs, too. Only once did our participation cause a stir among the audience. We were in the midst of a revival campaign. The evangelist preached well, the crowds were overflowing, and the Spirit of God moved mightily upon the hearts of the congregation. The chorus and testimony time seemed charged with the presence of God. As children, we, too, felt God was in our midst and in our childish way we opened our hearts to worship Him. David was always soft to the Spirit of God, and on this night he must have been moved to show God how much he loved him. He shouted for one of his favorite songs: "Let's sing, 'Old MacDonald'."

There was a moment of stunned silence. Seldom was my father speechless, but what could a preacher say to his son's sincere request. No one dared laugh; only the pastor could direct his little parishioner into a better way of expressing his love to God. The audience waited. Dad recovered quickly, a big smile told us he knew how to satisfy David: "Son, let's sing a song that everyone knows, 'Jesus Loves Me.' " One big smile of relief seemed to envelop the people; lustily they sang out for the children. David's grin and loud singing told the people that Jesus loved him, this he knew. "Old MacDonald" was left sitting in the barnyard.

When we weren't in church, we were accompanying Dad and Mother while they were about some other business for their heavenly Father. During the summer months we looked forward excitedly to Saturday evening each week. This was our night out on the town with a group of parishioners to hold street meetings in front of the local bank at the corner of Main Street and Philadelphia Avenue.

We got our baths early and the boys slicked themselves up in case they might be seen by certain girls. I could never understand why they even bothered—they always tried to escape from being seen publicly. I know, because we little people were boosted up on the wide window sills of the bank, and from our vantage point we could see the older kids edging away from the group, the pastor's sons leading the way. I was in third grade before I became too proud to be seen with the "holy rollers" and started edging *my* way to the opposite corner.

For a long while, Tuesday nights were highlights in our lives. Dad had been asked to preach once a week in the country church of Hellertown. We'd come home from school, hurry with our homework and then, one by one, we'd approach Dad with a request to please the heart of any preacher: "Dad, may I go with you when you go to preach tonight?" Dad was honestly too heavenly minded to see through our earthly desires. We didn't fool Mother! She knew Dad loved ice-cream cones as much as his children did, and when we passed through the town of Patton, Dad would be sure to stop at the drugstore. It became so automatic with Dad we didn't even have to plant the idea in his head. In fact, we stopped there so often Dad got the burden to establish a Pentecostal church in Patton and finally started street meetings in the town.

One of our most cherished memories of Barnesboro is the family vacation. Where else would a minister like my father take his family but to a religious camp? Dad had arrived in the eastern district just in time to offer his services for locating land to erect a camp. Not far from Barnesboro they found an ideal spot, just off a main highway. What really enticed them was an underground mountain stream that flowed unceasingly out of a sloping hill right into the middle of the gounds. Living Waters Camp became our annual vacation land, not just for the spiritual good, but also because the two weeks were a very economical vacation for our family of seven.

Together with other ministers and laymen Dad worked to clear acres of land for a tabernacle and rows of tents. Over the spouting water they built a pump house, and I believe that pump house still supplies water for the camp. When the appointed time arrived, they spread fresh sawdust and straw on the dirt floor of the tabernacle, donned their best suits and gathered together for a time of spiritual refreshing.

In those days, we children were unaware we were being cheated out of our real identity; we happily accompanied the adults to camp. Eventually they did provide a program for youth during the adult camp. This is the time we looked forward to. While our parents attended a morning Bible study session we gathered in two rented one-room schoolhouses just at the edge of the camp grounds for religious instruction. In the afternoon, while the adults attended services again, we were permitted to play ball—only after we had assured the ministers this in no way would keep us out of the evening services.

David looks back to the camp he attended during his eleventh year as the year of his calling into the ministry. It was during the war years and Dad's salary had somewhat diminished because men had been inducted into the service and some families had moved away to take jobs in defense plants. Dad was able to secure a work scholarship for Dave and, in spite of the fact that one of the jobs was doing dishes, he wanted to attend.

As David approached his teens he lost all the candy-bakery-store weight and now he suddenly looked more like a bean pole. He viewed his skinny physique with disgust, especially when he looked at Jerry with his dimples and curly blond hair. The girls will never make eyes at me," he worried to himself. He affected to me manliness sporting his green corduroy jacket from morning to night to cover up his skinny arms. After a while the jacket became a source of humiliation. It wasn't easy to hit a ball with a jacket on and with sweat rolling down his body. No captain wanted a teammate who couldn't roll up his sleeves and give the ball a good whack.

Being a failure in sports wasn't nearly as bad as watching the girls bypass him for his handsome younger brother. The jacket remained his cover-up until the graduation excercises on the last night of camp. The preacher's sermon caught David's attention: "I don't care how fat or skinny you may be—God can use you."

David sat on the edge of his seat waiting to hear more: "God is calling some young person tonight. He wants to use you to reach thousands of souls for Christ's sake. All he asks of you is that you come and present your bodies as a living sacrifice for Him. You are never too young to make this consecration to God. Come, give yourself to God."

Never before had the words of a sermon struck him as those did. Oh, he loved God and he knew God loved him; but to think that God could *use* him, that God actually *wanted* him—skinny and all!

David couldn't wait until the altar service. At the invitation to go forward, he jumped up, ran down the isle and flung himself down on the sawdust and straw. With arms raise up toward the heavens he cried out: "Jesus use me. Put your hand on my life." A nearby minister placed his hand upon David's head and prayed: "Lord, do use this young boy for your service. Let him never lose this zeal and desire to serve Thee that he feels so strongly this night."

Hours later David got up, his face beaming. He had received the "call"—the very same call that Granddad had once received, the same call that Dad had received. No one knew that evening, not even David, how God would use him; but from that moment on he was ready and willing to answer yes to whatever God asked him to do.

Dad was more than pleased to see David's desire for the ministry. He presented him with the book, Foxe's Book of Martyrs, with the solemn advice: "David, God always makes a way for a praying man. You may never be able to get a college degree, you may never get rich, but God always has and always will make a way for a praying man—so pray, David."

9
Personalized Prayer

THE WAY OF LIFE our parents taught and lived before us had the Word of God as its blueprint and was buttressed by their fervent prayers. The only misplaced "bricks" in our foundation of faith were our church's traditions. Over the years, we all learned how to determine what traditions were Scriptural and what were man-inspired. Putting the *do's* and *don'ts* of our upbringing in their correct perspective happened when we permitted the faith of our parents to work for us and not against us. I discovered the path of Truth wasn't really unreachable, though at times I confused the only Way with our side roads of tradition. Because in our thinking we had been trained to view life in the light of eternity, and because we were instilled with the knowledge of our rights as creatures of God to have direct communication with Him, we were able, if we so chose, to know what was the Way, the Truth, and the Life.

My father regarded the Scriptures as the only guideline for living, and he revered prayer as the greatest force upon the earth. He studied many hours, searching the Scriptures and seeking to know how rightly to divide the Word. But it was Dad's prayer life that made him a forceful and annointed preacher. Dad believed through prayer miracles were wrought in the lives of men: the transferring of men's minds from evil to good, the healing of diseased bodies, and the moving of God's heart on behalf of His creation. He depended on prayer to bring his spirit into communication with God's spirit and thereby receive guidance from God, receive a divine annointing to preach the Truth, and give power to live a godly life. Such a mighty way of life, he could not help but share.

The knowledge of the Word and of communication with God was

instilled in us from the moment we were born. We were only a few days old when Dad took us into his arms and dedicated our lives to God before the altar of the church. From that day forth we were laid, then sat, on pews, learning the Scriptures and learning how to pray. When other children were going off to dreamland to the sound of lullabies, we slumbered to the sound of our father's sermons and the prayers of the congregations. As we grew older we began to take part in the services. The sermons and the praying were as exciting as the songs. We all knew long before we heard the word *astronaut* that man would be going to the moon. This was all part of Dad's sermons on prophecy, and our church was fifty years ahead of society in knowing the importance of self-expression. Our prayer service, which followed every worship service, was a concert of prayer made audible to God by the entire congregation, including the children. It was at these altars we received a spiritual experience.

All five of us children knelt at these altars. We learned to pray by watching and listening to our elders. We poured out our love to God with childish expressions of worship and tears of happiness from the warmth we felt within. Many times we cried tears of repentance, thanking God for his mercifulness.

There is something unexplainable about what happens at these altars. We like to pray there, we wanted to. As children we did it without questioning; then we were teen-agers and we wondered why everyone prayed so loud, or why Sister So-and-So had to sound like a rooster. We still went to the altar to pray, but we did it as quietly as possible, hoping to keep the over-all volume down. It never helped!

Family prayer was the "mortar" for our family togetherness. When the time for prayer came, Mother dispatched the nearest child to round up the others. The entire neighborhood became accustomed to our prayer criers bellowing out: "Come on home, it's time to pr-a-ay!" Immediately we stopped playing and headed for the living room. Our parents never had to explain the importance of prayer; the very fact it was done daily, without fail, made us respect the sacredness of family prayers. I don't recall anyone of us refusing to join the family in prayer. I think we all rather cherished these moments because it was one of the few togetherness projects we shared as a family.

Mother used a variety of ways for hiding the Word within our hearts. Had she continually read from the *King James Version* I am sure we would have used the time to daydream. Instead, she challenged us with stories from simplified, Bible storybooks that made Bible characters come alive. Our heroes were Abraham, Joshua, David, Ruth, and Peter and a host of other Biblical men and women. We listened intently for Mother would be sure to ask questions on the lessons and each prided himself in being the smartest Bible scholar.

Then together we knelt, with the living-room sofa and chairs as our altars, and Dad prayed. He called us each by name before God. Chills of awesomeness would still our hearts as he prayed: "God, bless Juanita. May she always remember the Word she has learned around these altars. Help her to learn how to put it into practice in her life. Take David, Lord, and use him mightily for your Kingdom. May he realize nothing can be achieved by his own might or power, but only by your Spirit. And Jerry, Lord, watch over him. May your Spirit ever be with him, letting him know of your great love for him. Bless Ruth, and use her for your service as you have used handmaidens of old. And for our youngest, Lord, make him a preacher of the Gospel."

Blissfully, we scrambled up from our knees to go off to school or play, yet not for one moment did we doubt that God heard our father's prayer. When we were alone with our thoughts about life, we, too, talked with God, and our spirits cried out to Him: "God, we do want to serve you." It seemed such an easy committment to make when we were young.

I do believe ours was the only parsonage that could boast of personalized prayer, monogrammed with a razor strap. Dad never took a course in child psychology, but the very personal prayer sessions he used with his discipline methods proved he was master of the subject. His motto for these therapy sessions was: "Spare the rod and spoil the child," and he spared not because of our crying, either! Those who have married into our family are inclined to disbelieve me when I say we definitely were not the typical P.K. Rascals. They don't seem to know how much a three-inch-wide leather strap can hurt!

Dad used prayer both as a soothing balm and to make sure the whipping took. We just weren't allowed to cry and go off then, and pout. No! Our rebellious spirits were humbled even more when we were told to put our arms around Dad's neck and say, if we *could* in our grief, "I love you, Daddy. Forgive me for disobeying." Then Dad would tell us, "I love you too, but now we must ask God to help you overcome your stubbornness."

We had some classic spankings in our Hall of Disfame, one of the most shameful being prompted by David, the ringleader of mischief. It seems David would never accept his responsibility for doing dishes. "That's a woman's job," he'd fuss, every time it was the boys' turn. Mother felt this was the least the boys could do to help in our busy household, so his fuming went unnoticed, until he took matters into his own hands. "I'll show them," he told Jerry one morning, "I'm leaving home and they'll be sorry they ever made me do a dish." Off David traveled. He roamed the streets until his feet ached, then wearily, he climbed Old Baldy hoping to see some effect of his rebellion upon the household.

"He'll be back," Mother had confidently informed us, but supper went by and still no sign of David. The four of us formed a posse and searched the neighborhood. Finally, Dad decided to ride around, hoping to find David before dark. David looked down and saw the beginnings of our anxiety and smugly rejoiced to himself, "I'll bet they'll appreciate me after this."

He stayed out long enough to give us all a good scare and then came marching triumphantly down the hill, ready to receive the Prodigal Son's welcome; but there was no fatted calf, and no merrymaking. We all, under instructions from the higher-ups, ignored the one who had dared to punish us for his act of rebellion. Though Mother knew he was tired and hungry, we offered not a morsel of food. Dave sat brooding on the front-porch swing while we hung around sufficiently out of sight, waiting for the action to start. Finally, Dad walked out the front door and said, "Alright, son, up to the room." As always, King Solomon's discipline theory brought about a painful, but peaceful settlement.

Dad emphasized the importance of prayer in the church by having prayer in every meeting with members of the congregation. No matter if it were a board meeting, or dinner in the home of a parishioner, Dad took time for prayer.

The invitations to homes of church members were also occasion of togetherness for our family, thanks to such wonderful people as the Smiths, the Greenaways, the McGees and the Boyles. Going to their homes was better than going to the finest of restaurants. We were greeted royally and the banquets they spread were fit for a king's family. After the supper hour, the grown-ups met in the living room to talk over spiritual matters while we played together with our friends. When Mother announced: "We're going to pray now," we knew it was time to go home. Dad never left a home, no matter how long or short the visit, unless he had prayed God's blessing upon the household.

Prayer during board meetings was primarily to seek God's direction in church matters, but David recalls one time in Barnesboro when Dad used prayer for protection. It is a known fact that even saints have disagreements, possibly because we are never as saintly as we think we are. When the disagreeable are the carnal-minded, the Word usually corrects their evil tendencies, but when the disagreeable are the self-righteous, the Word cannot penetrate their wall of pride. As the Barnesboro church prospered and grew, new members were added and, even though Dad maintained a strict membership code, somehow those goats always managed to mingle with the sheep.

We children recognized them as people who shouted the loudest or who proudly displayed gifts of the Spirit they had received—in better days, no doubt! If I were to say today, "Remember the lady who forever interrupted Dad's sermons with her utterance in an unknown language?" we all would say her name simultaneously, for she was the source of trouble. Her gossip about the pastor and the church members knew no bounds: discord reigned supreme because of her malicious tongue.

In the midst of these troublesome days, Dad called for a special board meeting. He had heard that the dear sister had so influenced two of the board members that they threatened, "We'll beat the tar out of the pastor. How dare he call us carnal and self-righteous and say our gifts are not of God!" David overheard Dad tell Mother, "They're out to get me this time, but they can't hurt me. I've got God to protect me."

David wanted to tell Dad, "You've got God *and* me. I'll be there to help you." But he knew Dad would only thank him for his concern and tell him God would take care of him. Dave just wasn't sure but what Dad might have to go through peril like the Apostle Paul, and he meant to see that Dad was rescued from such tribulations. From the basement he armed himself with a football helmet and a rusty sword left from the previous tenants; then, with lightning speed, he ran through the back alleys, beating Dad and the board to the church.

By huddling in the coal bin where the cold-air return from the sanctuary would be just above him, Dave was able to hear every word being said. He heard the footsteps of Dad, then the slow heavy pace of six men behind him. They were gathering at the altar. He heard Dad's strong, deep voice: "Brethren, I think we need to begin this board meeting with prayer around the altar." The seven men knelt and Dad prayed. He peppered his prayer with all kinds of Scriptures about the dangers of touching God's annointed; he reiterated the tragedy of those who murmured and complained in the Israelite congregation; then he asked God to have mercy on the Achans of his congregation. Though that board meeting ended with brotherly hugs and David was able to put away his weapons, the undercurrent of gossip remained because of the sister's insistence of her righteousness and repeated demonstrations in almost every service of her "many gifts of the Spirit."

When problems arose within the family or the congregation, Dad literally agonized before God in the secret of his closet. Both he and Mother had their personal prayer time each day, and we took for granted the sounds of fervent prayer flowing from the lips of our parents, permeating the house with the presence of God. We walked quietly, as if on holy ground, when we heard either of them pray. If we tiptoed past their bedroom, we could hear our own names mentioned. It never failed to fill me with an awesome fear of God. It gave me all the more desire to serve God with all my heart and it expressed to me how much Mother and Dad really loved us. To this day I can feel the potency of those prayers; it is as if I can still hear my name being called before God. I am sure it was those prayers that made us aware of God's great love and personal concern for us and that kept burning within us the desire to live for Him.

It was during these hours in my father's Gethsemane that he prayed for strength to withstand the darts of Satan. Unfortunately, in those days, my father had no sort of recreation except for an occasional walk through the hills. Dad kept true to one of the Pentecostal traditions—exercise profiteth little—which was interpreted to mean it is a sin to waste time exercising the body. For my father, it was a sin *not* to exercise, for he badly needed a release from the many tensions of pastoring.

He kept up his strenuous task of shepherding the flock, ignoring his loss of weight and strength and the gnawing pain in his stomach, praying that God would send him to another congregation. He hoped some other pastor could show the dear sister the error of her ways; he felt he had done all he could.

When the answer to his request arrived, it came from such an unexpected source, and was such an unexpected answer, that Dad refused to recognize the call as coming from God. Actually, it was not a direct invitation from a church but a plea for help from the son of one of the Barnesboro parishioners, who told Dad of the little church he was attending and how badly they needed faith-building sermons such as Dad preached.

An invitation from a smaller church that had endured greater discord than Barnesboro seemed a direct contradiction to the love of God for his children. Dad commented to Mother: "I don't think God expects me to take the family into such a situation." For the second time in my father's life, he did not pray about the call, he simply threw the letter in the wastebasket.

Several months later he lay dying as the result of internal bleeding. Steadfastly, Dad had refused to believe he was seriously ill; now there seemed no hope that he would live. The five of us lined the stairs leading to the second floor waiting for the sound of the ambulance. Our hearts were frightened and broken as we heard Mother praying that God would spare Dad's life while Dad could be heard calling out strange things. "Why does he keep talking about the beautiful flowers," I kept asking Nan. " 'Because he's unconscious," was her bewildering reply. We watched with tears streaming down our cheeks as the funeral director, who was also Dad's friend, tenderly carried Dad down the stairs. David sobbed as if his heart would break; he put his arms around Mother and told her, "It's okay, Mom, if anything happens to Dad, I'll go to work and take care of you." Even through her tears Mother gratefully whispered, "Thank you, son."

The prayers of the congregation Dad had so unstintingly served for ten years brought about a miraculous deliverance. The doctor's only comment: "It had to be God," verified this fact.

Dad came home from the hospital firmly believing that his trial of sickness could have been avoided had he answered *yes* to that invitation from the small church. He vowed he never again would refuse a call until he had learned whether it be of God.

No sooner had he made his promise than the persistent young man again wrote, urging Dad to reconsider pastoring his church. This time Dad sat down at his desk to make an immediate reply: "Yes, if your church board wants me for a candidate, please set a date and I'll be there."

10

Just Some Suburb

WE WERE all excited about moving. I had suddenly become a VIP in my school because of the great occasion. Not many kids in Barnesboro ever moved—it was sort of a phenomenon.

"Where are you moving to?"

"Oh, near Pittsburgh,"

"Yeah, but what's the name of the place?"

"Oh, just some suburb."

The four of us (Don hadn't started school) went through the same torture with our classmates. We simply couldn't bring ourselves to say we were moving to Turtle Creek. Why, that sounded even more countryish than Barnesboro! And here we were, bragging that we were moving to the city. We became followers of the great white lie. To this day we all refer to Dad's pastorate there as Pittsburgh; or if we are in a more benevolent mood, we say T.C.

The very name dampened our anticipation of moving. Who could enjoy living in a town by that name! Had we known the shocking facts Dad purposely left out of his description of the town and church, we certainly would have vetoed the move by a unanimous vote. Only the *description* of our new abode sounded worse than the *name*. After a grand tour of T.C., we all expressed the same feeling: "No wonder Dad threw the first invitation in the wastebasket." We wished he had done the same with the second letter.

Yet, just as Paul felt compelled to answer the Macedonia call, so Dad felt compelled to answer the T.C. call. "I can do all things through Christ who strengtheneth me," was my father's promise from God that he could tackle the Turtle Creek charge.

Turtle Creek *was* "all things". It was a dirty town nestled among

102

dirty Westinghouse factories. It was a church located in the flood area of the town and situated almost underneath a railroad trestle. It was an apartment parsonage above the sanctuary with no place for children to play. It was a congregation numbering only forty people. It was a decrease in salary for Dad of fifty percent, *and* it was misery.

Until the day Dad made his decision to move, we children knew nothing about our parents' plans. Now we had no choice but to enter the drudgery of packing. Nan supervised the final organizing while Mother and Dad went to T.C. to make arrangements for moving.

Dad had made one stipulation before accepting the pastorate. He would not raise his family in the apartment that was to serve as a parsonage; however, the income of the church was so limited that it meant Dad must sell the Barnesboro house and invest in another. To his dismay, he discovered houses cost three to four times as much as the house we owned. Our home would provide money for only a down payment on a house in T.C.

Nevertheless, Dad knew the hardships of the T.C. ministry would be great enough without subjecting his family to poor living conditions. So the search for another home began. It became THE prayer request at our family altar.

Mother and Dad drove up and down the hills looking at houses listed in the newspaper and suggested by church members. They narrowed the choice down to two homes, one in the valley and one on the steepest hill. Dad took us all along for the final closing. Neither house could compare to our home in Barnesboro, but the house in the valley seemed the lesser of the two evils; at least that's what Dad and Mother felt. As for me, I simply hated the dark, dismal house. Thoughts of moving into *that* house filled me with dread. With tears of anguish I made my prayer without ceasing: "Please, God, find something better for us."

I'm sure my parents must have made the same request secretly, for just a few days before Dad had to finalize the purchase of that house, a member suggested a house in another area. "It's on Albert Street, which is only two blocks in length, but I don't know which house is for sale."

With this tidbit of information, Mother and Dad drove up T.C.'s more affluent hill and found the street. Driving slowly down the two blocks, glancing at each house could not possibly reveal which house was for sale, so Mother said, "Stop here. I think I'll ask the people in this house if they know which one is for sale."

An older woman answered the door bell of 342, where Dad had parked the car. "Yes," she replied to Mother's inquiry, "there is a house for sale, just across the street."

"Would you happen to know what price they are asking?" This was Mother and Dad's greatest concern. They felt the homes on this hill would surely cost more than those they had already seen.

"Well, I'm not quite sure. I heard they are asking around seventeen thousand dollars."

"Oh dear," Mother couldn't hide her disappointment. That was far above the amount they could afford.

"You know, it is strange you should stop and ask me about a house. My husband and I are thinking of selling our home and retiring, however, we are only in the talking stage. . . ." Her voice trailed off. Mother waited with suspense. The words of this woman struck a feeling of unrealness—of being in a dream and about to wake up and find the dream true.

Finally the woman spoke: "But we just might sell now if you are really interested."

"I'll get my husband." The reality of the entire happening suddenly hit Mother. God had led them to the very house he had wanted them to have! Mother was sure they would buy this woman's house. She walked to the car, her face beaming with the conviction that they were home. "Honey, we've found the house. But this isn't the one we've been looking for."

Dad had been anxiously waiting for Mother's seemingly unending conversation to cease. Now he found Mother's confidence a bit aggravating. He was tired of house hunting: his patience had long since worn thin with such a mundane chore.

"What do you mean, we've found the house? Is this house for sale or isn't it?"

Mother loves to be mysterious about a happening, especially when she feels sure about its coming to pass. "You'll see," she answered Dad. "Just come and talk with these people."

The outcome of that unscheduled conversation, between the owners of 342 and my parents, was our taking over a house again, this time as the owners, while the occupants moved next door. Only the neighbors thought it unusual for the Millers to sell their house and move to a rented apartment directly next door, before deciding where they would retire.

Moving to a city from a quiet community was like going from night to day. If you considered the dirt, it was like going from day to night. Houses were closer together, yards much smaller, and life in general moved at a faster and more aggressive pace.

We had arrived positive we would never like T.C. It was a sacrifice we were all making for the sake of the Gospel, but we were definitely going to rise to the occasion—we wouldn't dare let the city folks get the best of us. Mother and Dad, of course, weren't hampered by vain pride; they wholeheartedly took to city people and city life. But we five "righteous" disdainfully held ourselves apart from city slickers who boldly presented themselves to us for our friendship. The truth of the matter was we were so uninformed about city life that we were downright ashamed, and we weren't accustomed to such aggressiveness and such worldliness that seemed to thrive all around us. It took us sometime before we took off our self-righteous wrappings and admitted we were city P.K.'s.

While Mother went about settling us in the new house, Dad shut himself into his study, searching out the Scriptures and asking God for sermons that would change the defeated course of the church to one of victory. Nan, David, Jerry, Don and I went about making new discoveries.

When I was being raised, the words of Christ: "I pray not that thou shouldest take them out of the world, but that thou shouldest keep them from evil" (John 17:15), were interpreted by Pentecostal believers to mean we were to live among the sinners yet keep ourselves almost totally out of the affairs and pleasures of the world. We did not believe Christianity called for ascetic living. Taking part in the ways of the world was to be carnal minded, so we were not to walk the way of the flesh. Because no set rules were listed in our doctrines, the idea as to what was sin and what was not varied among the saints, and varied with time.

My parents, during my teen years, tried to guide us gently but firmly. We children were permitted the friendship of classmates, but not the privilege of attending all their pleasures. Sports made the *Do* list, but never movies or amusement parks. Modern clothes passed inspection, but not make-up nor jewelry. Our social activities were limited to church affairs and occasional birthday parties of our neighborhood friends.

Everyday I was shocked into the realization that we children had lived a very sheltered life in Barnesboro. I never had imagined a world such as this: there were school activities galore and an abundance of worldly friends who didn't think it strange to associate with a Pentecostal preacher's kids. Even the church had an organized youth group that reveled in socials (never in the church basement, of course), picnics, Christmas pageants, choirs (no robes), and none of the kids thought anything of taking part in school sports or clubs. Some, I was appalled to learn, visited amusement parks.

Paths of pleasure beckoned me on every hand, but I hesitated to take any one of them for fear they might be leading to destruction. When I politely said no to their invitations, my new friends indignantly retorted, "Well, you sure are a goody-goody. Too good for us heathens, is that it?"

That roused my English bullheadedness: I decided to behave like a normal city dweller, so down the road of worldliness I walked. My first daring experience was with a group of other fifth-grade girls who invited me to join their newly formed club, which was still unnamed. Delighted to be with the "in" girls, I became an active member, even suggesting "hubba-hubba" as the most daring name I could think of. At our meetings I became versed in the knowledge of Hollywood movie stars via the media of paper cutouts, but as I listened to the intimate gossip my friends seemed to know about these famous people they so adored, I came to the conclusion that my Bible heroes were much more interesting people. The more I learned about the stars the less I desired to go to the movies. They surely didn't seem worth my being condemned to hell, at least not so early in my life.

One sinful deed surely leads to another. I had been warned, and it was so. Three teen-agers who lived next door begged us to enter their games, which required the throwing of dice. We were permitted to play games; at Christmas Mother and Dad carefully chose games that each of us particularly enjoyed, but not before Mother censored them, substituting spinners for the evil dice. However, since our parents had no say over the neighbors' games, I nonchalantly threw dice in their homes and respectably twirled spinners in ours. It wasn't until my high-school days that I learned why dice were on the condemned list. Fortunately, by then, my stealthy handling of them hadn't uncovered any hidden gambling instincts so I never fell prey to that vice.

While sports were still on the condemned list, they became the worldly downfall of David and Jerry. They obediently viewed the games from afar and this sufficed while they were novices about the things of the world. A year later, when we were all sophisticated city people, the boys boldly confronted Dad for some answers: "Why can't we go to the games? Is playing ball in a stadium a sin?" It was one of the few times the boys questioned the *Do-Not* list, and they stood waiting for Dad's answer. "I guess there really isn't any sin involved," he said. "You may go on one condition; these ball games must never keep you from attending church." The crisis was over and with the greatest of ease. The boys were elated. T.C. wasn't so bad after all. In fact, T.C. was the greatest! And Dad, too!

Even the most innocent of us got himself entangled in the snares of the world. Cunningly, Don purported his vice to be an educational program, all the while blackmailing his brothers and their friends with pictures his photography club had snapped and developed. He finally forsook this evil for the pleasures of miniature golf and, in the process, had to embezzle the photographic club's funds in order to pursue his new interest. Squandering the club's 75 cents didn't help Don's image as a P.K. and so ended his enterprising days. He quickly mended his ways and turned to a more useful, but less profitable, profession—the ministry.

He converted his room on the third floor into a chapel, practicing his song-leading and sermon abilities on David and Jerry. They urged him on and Don never seemed to notice he was the only one singing and praying. They sat up and took notice of his sermons, though: their little preacher brother began revealing their sins that he had heard them whispering when they thought him asleep. From then on, Don got to take part in quite a few of the pleasures of the world with his brothers.

Don recalls vividly an incident that forever taught him to practice what he preached. He had made arrangements to meet a girl friend in the city and treat her to the delights of Kenneywood Park —Pittsburgh's largest amusement park. Don had made the 45-minute trip by streetcar before, with Dave and Jerry, but this was his first venture into the city alone. Because of his destination, he couldn't bring himself to ask permission to make the trip alone; he simply went, never thinking his deed might be found out. He arrived at the meeting point a half hour early. A tent across the street drew his attention, especially when he discovered it was sponsored by a healing evangelist. He walked across the street and into the tent to wait out the time in a more secure location than the busy street corner. The day had been windy to begin with and now the wind seemed to blow with hurricane force. Don was glad for the safety of the tent until suddenly, with a loud swish, the large tent lifted from its stakes and began descending, like a parachute, down upon the seats.

Thankfully, Don had chosen a seat just inside the door and easily made an escape. He ran back to the street corner, trembling and almost in tears, realizing had he been sitting in the middle of the huge tent, he could have been killed. Don met the girl and they had their thrills on the rides, but Don's mind was not at peace. Conviction settled down upon his heart just as the tent had slowly settled on the ground. He had to make a confession to ease his mind. Just telling his girl wasn't enough. A convenient confessional box stood nearby: it was marked TELEPHONE. He paid his dime and made his confession to his father: "Dad, this is Don."

"Where are you?"

"In Pittsburgh!"

"What are you doing there? How did you get there?"

Out came the story of Prodigal Son Number One. The lecture Don received wasn't half as bad as the lesson he learned. From then on, Don wanted to keep his record clean and that episode was as close to rebellion as he ever got. He planned to be a minister and he wanted to be as good a one as his father.

Many of my classmates expected me to be somewhat different simply because I was a P.K., and because my father was the minister of a church that was considered a bit fanatic—and that's putting it mildly. Being a P.K. never really bothered me. In fact, I took great pride in boasting that my father was a minister. Once a ninth-grade teacher asked the class what we thought was the more important job in the country and when she came to me I promptly said, "A minister's." We were all wrong, according to her thinking. "Garbage collectors are needed most," she informed us. The entire class laughed. It sounded funny to them, but not to me. "No wonder she thinks that," I whispered to my girl friend, "she's a heathen. She doesn't even go to church."

Sometimes, though, I used to cringe when classmates in school said, "Hey, your Dad pastors that Holy Roller church, huh?"

"No he doesn't!" I could offer no defense other than an emphatic denial. I knew very well why we were called *that* name and I wished to heaven a few folks would be a bit less demonstrative in their expression of worship. The praying around the altars (concert praying Dad called it) I didn't mind too much, but when Sister So-and-So burst out like a rooster crowing, it left me embarrassed and bewildered. I wished Dad would teach her to yield to the Spirit more quietly, or else keep the church windows shut during the services. Some of my classmates lived just across the street from the church.

The feeling of being different plagued me throughout my teen years. I did not want to be different, nor did I want to be a sinner. I loved God and wanted to serve Him. So, like many teens in my church, I struggled with what seemed an impossibility—trying to relate myself to my world and to the one that surrounded me.

Aware of our fellowship needs, Mother and Dad made an all-out effort to offer us a satisfying social life. Mother personally supervised the youth group, indoctrinating us with Scripture that would guide us to the right pathway of life. She also took time to chaperone picincs, and several times a year a social was held. A few pleasures that the Barnesboro membership frowned upon were gradually eliminated from the condemned list: after a while we all could attend the school sports events and the boys were given freedom to sight-see Pittsburgh. (They bought more peanuts at the zoo than any other preacher's kids in Allegheny County.) To keep us happy at home, Dad dug into his limited income to provide us with a Ping-Pong table, and he nailed up a basketball net on the garage.

For the boys, these activities were enough, for they were the very things they liked to do. Working after school and on Saturdays kept them out of a great deal of mischief, I am sure, and it also gave them the satisfaction of being financially independent, which naturally provided a few extra privileges such as the use of Dad's car for dating.

But I, alas, a member of the weaker sex, had to find satisfaction in less adventurous activities. It was no fun watching my brothers and my friends go off for a good time with dates, so I sought what seemed a very natural escape—romance—to ease my loneliness.

Marriage happened to be one of my father's favorite subjects. He took delight in playing the role of Cupid and today there are several happily married couples who said I do thanks to Dad's art of matchmaking. Dad had definite ideas, some based on Scripture, plus a few prejudiced views from his proud English heritage.

Automatically, when I became interested in a fellow, Dad's philosophy would pop into my mind: "Look at his shoes. A man of breeding keeps them polished" (a hang-up from his Marine days). "Be not unequally yoked together. Of what stock is he? Does it harmonize with ours? Is he a gentleman? How does he treat his parents? Does he enjoy the things of life that you do? Does he serve God?" That was quite a list. I wondered—was there such a man for me?

When at last I reached my senior year in high school, I knew without a doubt, to just what extent I had been influenced—not just by Dad's pet theories—but by the total religious orientation to which I had been exposed. The choice to either accept or reject my parents' religion stood foremost in my mind. More than any other belief, the knowledge of a Creator who took a personal interest in each individual He created obscured the traditions that had troubled me, and it challenged me to trust my life in His hands. It was the beginning of finding my own identity, and it was a good beginning.

11

The Faithful Servant

IN THE LIBRARY of my home I have several black notebooks that I cherish. In them is page after page of my father's sermons which he wrote in longhand in the days before he owned a typewriter. Occasionally I read through one of his outlines; there doesn't seem to be a subject that Dad missed. The sermons contain all the reasons Dad lived as he did. I often wonder the reason for the move to T.C. The entire term there was a continual life of sacrifice for our parents. It meant Dad had to leave the *fat* years for the *lean* years. It meant, too, that Dad could not put away any savings for his retirement, much less think of sending any one of us to college.

Dad's sermons give the key to his willingness to make sacrifices for the sake of the Gospel. In almost every sermon he speaks of God's reward for the faithful servant—eternal life. Dad knew God would strengthen his weakened body for this call, and he joyously preached the reason why everyone succumbed to the temptations of acquiring worldly goods or fame; he ran the Christian race to win, always pressing toward the mark for the prize of his high calling. This hope of eternal reward sustained Dad so that he saw no reason to complain. My father kept his cool about our constant financial needs and he helped all of us keep our cool, too.

When it came to the work of the Lord, Dad had an exceedingly great amount of endurance. His patience with church members, board members, fellow ministers, and even with our parsonage economy, came from a bottomless well of understanding. He seemed to have greater patience with them than with such trivial things as misplaced household tools or with Mother when she cooked the same breakfast three days in a row.

111

The Bible does say tribulations worketh patience and, since Dad had many a day of trials, he was able to radiate a joyful and confident faith. His positive outlook upon the ministry helped him survive the pressures of the T.C. church. He saw neither small congregation nor small salary. His eyes beheld a hill just behind the church and far above the trestle. There on the corner of the block, where members of the town board and town merchants lived, was an empty piece of land no one wanted. The lot itself was a hill, rising as high as the houses next to it, and no builder wanted to conquer all the dirt and stone.

"Folks," Dad announced after preaching for a solid year on launching our faith, "when you leave the church today, look up to the hill above, and know that God is going to put us there someday. That corner is seen from every hill in our city. We'll be a shining light to the glory of God."

It took five years of preaching, patience, faith and giving. Today there stands a red-brick colonial church built on solid rock. The town laughed when Dad hired a bulldozing company to knock down the hill of earth. "You'll never dig a foundation out of that stone," they scoffed. The huge shovels easily dug the dimensions for the basement and had to stop. They had no need to go any farther—they couldn't—below was all solid rock. Upon that rock they built the church.

One of the members of that church was Brother David Morgan, the very man who had suggested they try for the Barnesboro pastorate. It is his granddaughter, Gwen, who became David's wife. About such happiness it is said, "It's a small world." My father regarded such a coincidence as the hand of God in the affairs of man.

Such extraordinary occurrences were not unusual in our home. We had been in T.C. two years, and the financial problems of our household were still no better. We children were getting older and our needs greater; Dad's car was wearing out and had to be replaced. Things looked desperate. Then a woman evangelist who came from another Pittsburgh suburb to take part in Dad's revival campaign magnanimously offered David a job in her husband's grocery store. We knew she had been a God-sent messenger. Eventually Jerry went to work with Dave and together they helped to boost the family income.

That year was Nan's senior year. She, too, found a job and was able to buy her own clothes and other necessities. I remember her saving all her change so that she could go to college. We were all forced to learn lessons in economizing. I was too young to work, except for an occasional baby-sitting job; but I learned I could help ease the tension simply by not asking for things I could do without.

The scarcity of money was the second most important factor influencing the *Don't* list. Now it loomed like an impossible mountain blocking Nan's dream of going away to college. All her silver and copper coins could not begin to make her dream come true, and neither could Mother and Dad work magic with their budget, so Nan chose to attend our denominational Bible school, where tuition was much less than at secular colleges.

For Dave, the parsonage was never a cage. Remembering Granddad's dramatic ministry, Dave saw beyond the life of sacrifice to a life of adventure. The call to preach still burned within.

Dad was proud to see his firstborn son desiring to follow in his footsteps. He kept David's flames of zeal burning by taking time to instruct him how to prepare a sermon: "Read, then pray, then prepare a good outline."

Dave took Dad's advice and put it to work at an early age. When he was sixteen he felt ready to prove himself a preacher. He approached Dad with a proposition: "Dad, I think I'm ready to preach —thought maybe you'd let me preach for you first. Then do you think you could line up a few services in some of the nearby churches?"

"Son, you preach for me once, then we'll talk about the other." Dad believed in a man proving himself first, even his own sons.

Eyebrows arched heavenward when Dad announced to the congregation that Dave would be preaching at the evening service. We drove to church that night with quaking hearts. Dave had Dad's big Bible in his hand and sat cool and collected. Dad seemed more nervous than any of us.

"Do you have your outline, son?"

"Yes, Dad."

"Don't worry if your knees shake. Your first time, you're bound to be nervous."

"I'm not nervous, Dad."

"That's fine, son."

At last we were in the church. We sang, we prayed, the ushers took the offering. David's hour had come: "And now I am happy

113

to have my son, David, come and preach his first sermon. Your responsive *Amen's* will make it easier for him to preach."

With a firm step Dave strode to Dad's place behind the pulpit. He opened the big Bible, laid it down in front of him and looked up over the sea of eyes anxiously waiting for the pastor's son to speak.

We waited and waited. Not a sound came forth. His mouth hadn't even opened. He stood there, stiff and speechless, completely bound by fear. It took several moments for Dad to realize David's predicament. Quickly, he walked to Dave's side, turned to the congregation and said, "Join with me in prayer."

I thought Dad intended either to pray the benediction or deliver the message himself. Instead, he placed his hands on Dave's head and in his fervent voice prayed: "Father, David is bound by fear, and the author of fear is Satan. In the name of Jesus, I rebuke this spirit of fear. Release him that he may speak forth your Word. Now, son, preach," and Dad sat down in the front pew.

Dave's first sermon lasted all of fifteen minutes. No one remembered what he said, but we knew that he had won a lasting victory over the fear of facing an audience. No one knew, then, that this victory would help him to preach to larger audiences than either Granddad or Dad had ever faced.

After this preaching debut, Dad made preaching engagements for Dave among his surrounding minister friends. By the time Dave graduated from high school, he was anxious to enter the full-time ministry.

"Not before you've had some Bible training," Dad insisted. He remembered the wise advice of his own father.

Two years after Nan left, David set off for the same school almost penniless, but with an opportunity to earn his way and the promise of ten dollars a week, plus love letters to ease his lonely hours away from Gwen, his wife-to-be.

Dave decided after the end of his first year he was ready to begin his ministry. "Dad," he said, "I think I'll get some field experience, then go back to school." Dad couldn't find fault with David's conclusion. He had been sure of himself at the end of one year of schooling, too.

"All right, son, but find out from God in which field of labor you are most needed and suited."

David did just that and no one would believe him—especially

Mother. Even Father, with his patience and tolerance, wondered what had gotten into his seemingly level-headed son to choose ventriloquism as his method of preaching the Holy Word of God. "It's my father coming out in him, I guess," said Dad.

Mother let Dave know how she felt in no uncertain terms. "Dave, surely God has a better ministry for you than such childishness."

But already Dave had purchased all the equipment he needed to go on tour for children's revivals. "Don't touch that suitcase," he warned me one day when I curiously eyed a few of the magical tricks he had laid out on the dining room table. It sounded like such fun to me. There was a pitcher of milk, and when he poured it into a rolled up newspaper, it disappeared; and there was a stick that went limp when anyone else but Dave handled it.

Surprisingly, the very same ministers who had Dave in their churches to preach his first sermons were the ones to have him conduct his first children's services. Except for a few kinks that had to be ironed out in his presentation, Dave's new ministry was literally a howling success. He made the children laugh, he made them cry—best of all, he made them see that serving God was both serious and fun.

But for Mother's intercessory prayers, my brother Dave would probably be on his own television program doing some soft-pedaled Gospel preaching to all the children of the world. No reports of David's success could change Mother's mind. She prayed on. When at last Dave came home with the news that he planned to be a candidate for a small church not too far from Pittsubrgh, Mother began smiling again. The crisis was over.

It's one crisis after another in a parsonage—at least it was in our home—but the worst crisis Mother faced, and one that affected our entire household, was my father's continous bout with stomach ulcers. A thorough check-up in a Pittsburgh hospital revealed that Dad had several ulcers which periodically acted up. He was given some sound and stern advice by the doctor. "Reverend, you need to relax. Why not take up golf or fishing?"

This second scare seemed to bring Dad to his senses. He was more relaxed around the house and even shocked us by taking the doctor's advice to heart. Dad had used his days in the hospital to reflect upon his past and that of the family. One day as we sat talking in his study, he took a sheet of typing paper from his desk drawer and drew a large circle, and then in that circle another smaller circle, and in it he wrote the word GOD. Then he divided the outer circle into four parts, each centered on the inner circle. In each part he wrote a word: PLAY, FAMILY, CHURCH, STUDY. "This is the way it should be, a time for each, and all centered around God. Up until now, I haven't lived like this. All my time is for the church and studying, and now I see how my family has suffered. I've had the wrong perspective on the life of sacrifice, and I mean to make some adjustments.

For Don and me, who were now the only children at home, this was great news. For the first time in our family history, our parents could afford to take us on vacation with them, a real holiday vacation at a lake. I think it was during that week that I totally agreed with Dad's theory that being born into a minister's home is a rare privilege. "It's an education," he'd say, referring to the many people we met and the many problems we confronted and learned to cope with.

With such a God-given heritage, heaven forbid that I should desire worldly wealth; yet, from the moment I had heard the Biblical story of Ruth and Boaz, I determined to enlarge my initial blessing by adding wealth and romance to my life. I was willing to take heaven's consequences; after all, I reasoned with childlike logic, my name is Ruth, so surely this was in keeping with God's word.

"You'll see," I voiced, in most prophetic tones to the family. "I'll marry a man with lots of money and our troubles will be over!" I wanted to meet the man of my dreams just like the heroines in Grace Livingston Hill's novels. Always he was rich, of sterling character and very gallant—one who loved God but was worldly wise at the same time. His profession varied, but never, never was he a preacher.

I must admit, my anti-minister rebellion wasn't exactly the result of a deprived childhood. Looking back, I realize the great influence books had upon me. Mom and Dad read a lot, so it became a natural thing for us children to read, too. I read every book I could find; but it was Nan's romantic novels that introduced me to another world, an imaginative one, true, but one so much more enticing than life in a parsonage.

I firmly stuck to my dream until the day Dad announced he was moving to another charge. All my dreams of becoming a famous educator rapidly dispersed right before my eyes. No way developed, despite my efforts to remain in T.C., for me to take advantage of a scholarship at the University of Pittsburgh. It was as if I were forced to stand back while someone else took control of my life. It was an experience I had heard Mother and Dad speak of, but it was new and startling for me. I sought some assurance that giving up what seemed an opportunity for a life of success and fulfillment was, after all, God's plan for my life. I found the answer in the words of Christ: "But seek ye first the kingdom of God, and his righteousness; and all these things shall be added unto you" (Matthew 6:33).

12

No Other Way

GOD'S HAND moving in the affairs of our family was never more clearly visible than in our move to Scranton. We were taken to mountain top experiences and guided through the valley of death. We were able to rejoice through the darkest of days because His hand was there to sustain us, just as it had been for all the generations of the Wilkerson family.

The Scranton Assembly's history laid claim to our denomination's finest shepherds, each leading the congregation into green pastures. Dad felt greatly honored to follow in the footsteps of these esteemed brethren. The new challenge energized his weary body. He loved the new flock of sheep from the very beginning and if need be, he was ready to give his life for those he dearly loved.

He began his ministry in Scranton with an all-out revolutionizing program! He startled the dignified congregation into making a joyful noise unto the Lord. "Let's not drag the tempo folks. We aren't here to bury the dead, but to raise them up! Mrs. Owens, you just follow me with your good organ playing and we'll get along splendidly." The people smiled in spite of themselves and the old hymns of the church took on new life.

Right off, Dad instituted his musical trademark—chorus time—and the congregation loved it. "Why, our new pastor is like a bit of heaven come to us," a dear old saint rejoiced. "We haven't sung like this in years; it's like the days of the old time religion!"

Even the old Methodist Amen Corner came out of mothballs. The corner was off to one side of the chancel and many of the older saints gathered there for prayer and also sat there during the services. Their *Amen's* assured the pastor he was preaching the truth they liked to hear. Dad theorized from past experience that it was the younger generation who needed the assurance of what was truth more than the oldsters. "I appreciate that Amen corner, folks, but how are you folks out here in the main sanctuary accepting the truth?" From then on, the *Amen's* were spread out. That's the way my father liked it. *Amen's* tied the people in with the sermon.

Dad liked to brag about his congregation. "My people love the Word of God. They've been fed the choicest meat of the Scriptures. I really have to dig deep for new thoughts. There's no difficulty preaching to them; they sit there drinking it in as fast as I can preach it." Dad's greatest joy was when he was preaching and this was increased by a people who responded so readily.

In the early part of my father's ministry, he had flavored his preaching with the negative traditions of our church: don't attend worldly amusements: don't dress like the world; don't mingle with the world, and the usual list of *don'ts* we all could rattle off. He also practiced what he preached—that was the reason we suffered along with him. It must have been Dad's being an ardent student of the Word and a faithful prayer warrior that transformed his message to positive, heart-lifting expositions on living happy and useful lives for our creator.

No one who sat under my father's preaching should have fear of death. Dad made heaven so real, so glorious and so exciting that I made up my mind as a child I was going to heaven. He portrayed these days upon the earth as our passage through a short time in a labor of love to God, to be climaxed with a space trip to a city whose streets are paved with gold, where mansions stand among gardens of Eden and where Satan can never harm us. "Don't you think you'll be sitting on a soft cloud playing a harp. Heaven will be a busy place, it's capitol the heavenly Jerusalem. Talk about interplanetary space travel—why, we'll be traveling all over this universe. No longer will our knowledge be limited: God Himself will reveal His mysteries. And don't be surprised when you meet Kenneth Wilkerson playing a violin. That's been one of my great desires. I haven't achieved it here, but in heaven I'll be playing a violin!"

I wish all five of us had had the benefit of those Scranton days. The people greeted our family with open arms and treated even Don and me with love and respect. I don't recall any regular members finding fault with the preacher's kids, as congregations are so

119

apt to do. It made Don and me want to pitch in and give our best, too.

Because I had neither job nor scholarship, I spent my first year as an unpaid secretary to my father. My first job was doing the weekly church bulletin. Thanks to a handful of girls who had gone completely mad over my six-foot "little" brother, I had helpers enough to write out the addresses until Dad got the board to update our system by adding an Addressograph machine.

My greatest joy was taking charge of the youth group. Don assisted me by being faithful to my program and drawing all the young girls out to the weekly meetings. Naturally, the rest of the boys of the church followed the girls, so we had a fair-sized group ready to do whatever a leader suggested. Had the church seen the need for a religious educational director, I could have gone on indefinitely working in the church. In T.C., I had taught a group of nine- and ten-year olds just to see if I really wanted teaching as my career. Now, I was suddenly discovering parsonage and church life really appealed to me. I told Mother and Dad one day, "After this, all other work will seem boring." I sat in my father's study to type the bulletin while he and Mother were visiting. I found the atmosphere of that room where Dad studied, prayed and counseled was penetrating the shell of resentment I had built up against the hardships of the ministry. For the first time I began to wonder if teaching was God's plan for my life.

The day came when I knew I could no longer stay at home, living off my parents. I talked my situation over with them and they advised me to seek employment before going back to school. In those days not much work was available in Scranton. One day, after two weeks of looking, I sat at my father's desk, working on the weekly *Reminder*. I heard the newspaper hit the front porch with a thud and decided to stop for a rest and read the want ads. As I began to read, I suddenly felt that chill of awesomeness that grips me everytime the unknown is about to be revealed. A thought raced through my my mind: "There's a job for you in this paper." I read down through the ads, coming across one job that possibly I could fill, but it was thirty-five miles away and, of all things, in a honeymoon resort.

Resort sounded very worldly. I wondered what comments Mother and Dad would make. Surprisingly, when I told them I had called and was to be interviewed the next day, they promised to

120

pray that this would be the job. Of course, I was sure to tell them the owners were interested in me when our conversation revealed I knew their former manager. He was also a friend of my father, so any place his friend had worked would certainly be all right for his daughter.

I drove up to the Pocono's alone the next day, feeling sure I would get the job. Strickland's Mountain Inn did look worldly, but it also looked ritzy. Life would never be boring here, I thought, and it wasn't. I spent almost two years working there, enjoying every minute of it. I learned I could live my faith, even gain greater faith, be right in the world yet not partake of it and still have lots of fun being a Christian. I experienced a few firsts in the Pocono's. I met a young Catholic priest and did some research on the Catholic beliefs with his help. This prompted research on my own to see how scriptural were our beliefs. Dad took time out of his busy schedule to help me secure a car so that I could continue doing the bulletin for him on my day off. I made up my mind, after the third unsuccessful attempt to finish college, that God had other plans for my life.

I spoke to the youth group on finding God's plan for their lives and put myself on the spot by confessing I had taken Matthew 6:33 as a direct promise from God to me. I told them I had made up my mind to work for God first and was confident He would unfold His will for my life. This is what I had been taught all my life and now I was putting it to the test, really desiring this Bible inspired philosophy of life to be my now, not just that of my parents.

It was a telephone call from Margaret Milbrandt, the director of the childrens' department, that unveiled the next move in my new venture of faith. A week later I began working in Scranton for the same company Margaret worked for.

Once again I assumed my previous duties in the church, assisting Margaret in directing the children in the Christmas play.

Mother and Dad seemed genuinely glad to have me back home. Don had entered Bible college and, though they made no bones about enjoying their new freedom, they often expressed how much they missed us all, too. Nan had married and settled in Cleveland, Jerry had returned to T.C. to work in the grocery business and Dave had taken the pastorate in Phillipsburg.

Our family jam sessions, though greatly reduced in attendance, took on a more intimate nature. Now that I was over twenty-one, my parents seemed to be terribly worried about my love life. "Seems to me you are going out quite a bit with Bill," Dad commented one night after a Sunday evening service. That was Dad's way of asking about my intentions without seeming to pry, so I gladly clued him in.

"Nothing serious, Dad. Bill isn't going with anyone at the moment and neither am I. We're just one lonely old maid and one lonely bachelor keeping each other happy until our mates come along."

"Honey, we know you're concerned about your future and so far life has been disappointing. Mother and I are making your problem a matter of prayer and we believe God will direct you. You must seek God, too."

I knew exactly what was being recommended by Dad. The example of Mother and Dad seeking God had often stirred a hope that prayer might work for a young person, too; but to actually take even one half hour to pray, and to be so spiritual as to know how to pray in the Spirit, seemed too profound a method for a young girl to use in seeking her identity in life.

Yet, there stood our church, constantly beckoning to let its sanctuary be a refuge for me in my time of perplexity. Every time I passed the wide steps leading to the foyer, I felt compelled to try this way of praying. Then one day I came home from work, ate supper and then slipped over to the church. From that day forth until I found what I was seeking, I never missed a day, praying. What Apostle Paul said was true: "The Spirit also helpeth our infirmities: for we know not what we should pray for as we ought: but the Spirit itself maketh intercession for us" (Romans 8:26).

Life no longer seemed confusing—I knew who I was and where I was going. At last my faith was a reality, giving me inner peace and guidance. The searching was over with the simple act of trusting my life in the hands of my Creator. I had discovered at last what my mother and father believed and taught.

I did not think it strange to hear my father say at the supper table one spring evening in March, "Honey, I've been praying today concerning your future, and God told me you'll be meeting the man who'll be your husband in the *very near* future."

"Well, that sounds better than going off to Alaska," I retorted with a laugh. Dad was serious, that I knew; he never joked about receiving a message from God, but I was young in my probing of the mind of the Spirit for my life and it did sound a little preposterous. Most of me wanted to believe his marvelous revelation: part of me doubted it could happen so spectacularly to me.

Five months later I stood beside my knight in shining armor, happy beyond what I had ever comprehended happiness to be, while my proud father united us in marriage. Behind me stood my older brother, Dave, ready to give me away in marriage.

"So Matthew 6:33 really works," commented Lillian, my closest friend in the church. "I must remember that."

My husband, Don, and I settled in a three-room apartment in another part of the city. Dad seemed so thrilled that his prayer had been answered so quickly that he even went against his own advice to married couples and invited Don and me to live in the parsonage. I had been thoroughly indoctrinated with his marriage theories so we declined, but Dad still said, "I feel you both will live here in this parsonage someday."

"I hope that doesn't mean we'll both lose our jobs." I told Don after our visit with Mother and Dad. "That's how badly my father must miss us all."

"I don't see why," Don pointed out, "seems your brother Don is home every other week from school and David calls about every Sunday evening. Jerry and Nan keep in touch too. If we lived there, he'd be too busy to see us, anyway. This way, we see him twice a week and he takes time out to visit with us."

Those weekly visits became a ritual. Thursdays we went for supper and did the church bulletin. Sundays I dashed over after the sermon just as I always had, put the potatoes on to boil and started setting the table.

One particular Thursday the household seemed in an awful uproar. Dad had newspapers sprawled out on the kitchen table and there, staring out from the front page, was a picture of son number one looking like a frightened smalltown preacher trying to confront the wicked city of New York with a large black Bible. The caption read like a bizzare story that could happen only in some other family—never ours.

"What's gotten into David! Couldn't he be satisfied with being the only church in the Assemblies of God to have a television program!"

We found out what it was all about in short order. Dad made David tell it from the beginning. He had to know what had prompted David to make such a fool of himself and bring the wrath of two of our districts down upon him. "I only hope I'm respected enough to be able to save you from losing your ordination. There have been a lot of complaints, David, and I can't say that I blame them. You need to put more prayer into your actions."

After the initial shock subsided, we all put it from our minds. We weren't aware David had done just as Dad had said and was continuing to pursue his seemingly foolish notion. As so well told in David's book, *The Cross and The Switchblade*, God moved in the affairs of my brother until his vision became a reality. No one in our family had a thing to do with this venture, except that my husband and I drove David down for his first meeting with a committee of ministers in the Glad Tidings Tabernacle, our Manhattan Assembly. Any encouragement David received came only from heaven above. As the plan of God was revealed to David, we all began to regard his vision with a little more understanding. Dad remembered his words of prophecy that David would someday do a great work for the Kingdom of God.

A little talk with God made Dad confident., "David will come through this all—something good will come out of it if he depends on God to lead him." And, of course, Dad began a prayer campaign to made sure Dave did just that!

How well my father knew the importance of being led by God! He had come through so much and so victoriously because he had learned this secret of success very early in his ministry. Now he could look out the parsonage window and see a monument to his victories. In the place where once was a stately, but old and antiquated, stone church, a large brick colonial church stood, its steeple rising high in the heavens. The new church had been born of a vision too. No, Dad could not deny his son's vision. He had had visions, too, of a different nature, but no less and no more visionary than David's. I knew my father well enough to say he prayed that God would help David to see his vision through. He knew that for David there would be no greater joy.

For Dad, the vision for the Scranton church had been his crowning joy. He took over the pastorate not long after the board had voted to add to their present sanctuary. The parsonage had been moved to the corner lot to make room for the new addition, but Dad had a greater vision for the church.

He used the same God-given method to inspire the people to

seek those greener pastures that he used in T.C. As usual, he had a few stubborn "mules"—but Dad travailed with these faithless and inspired those of faith to claim the promises of God. He preached until the congregation had a mind to build. Soon the bricks were flying. Down came the old church and up went the new.

Dedication Day was glorious. Even the doubters bragged, "Look what we've done!" To themselves they mumbled, "Now, who's going to pay for it all?" (It certainly wouldn't be them, we knew!)

The spirit of revival reigned in our beautiful new church. Dad's vision beheld a growing and prosperous church. Greater victories seemed to fall to the right and to the left: the membership increased, the finances increased, and the town suddenly seemed aware of a going group of Pentecostals in their midst. Dad was invited to speak at a Presbyterian church to explain the meaning of the Holy Spirit coming on the day of Pentecost. The pastor's daughter met her husband in the sanctuary of the new church. His son, Don preached his first sermon from its pulpit. It was one of the first churches to hear of the Teen Challenge ministry.

In the midst of all these glorious victories stood "O ye of little faith." Doubt seems to spread faster than faith in a congregation. It could be because there are more members spreading this sin about. Dad had his doubters: "How are we going to pay such a debt? Is the money coming in? Did we really have to build such a *large* church?"

None of it inspired the preacher. "Let's believe God, He never starts a work that He does not see to the finish." Dad had walked the road of faith long enough to know and believe that God would not fail them. Dad did his best to get this truth across. Their doubt weighed heavily upon him.

On my visits home I noticed Dad's physical strength ebbing, and much worse, his spirit seemed so low my heart was distressed. "Something is wrong with my father," I repeatedly told my husband. Dad had had a serious operation just before I met Don and two-thirds of his stomach had been removed. We naturally thought he had not fully recuperated.

It is a thrill to have the unknown mysteriously revealed before it actually happens. It is not an unusaul occurence to those who have had the spiritual experience of living in the Spirit of God. Yet God in His compassion kept the knowledge of my father's slow death from us, even though so many tragic signs pointed toward it.

A year after his operation, Dad had gone visiting. Driving home, his car was hit from behind as he paused for a stop sign. It was a hard hit, not doing much damage to the car, but jolting Dad badly enough to cause him pain for several months.

The pain developed into severe headaches that brought on an unbalanced walk and loss of ability to focus his eyes. His doctor sent him to the hospital for X rays, but nothing seemed to be wrong. However, his blood pressure was so dangerously high the doctor ussued an ultimatum: "If you want to live, you must give up the ministry. Retire now and you'll add ten years to your life."

Only Mother and Dad shared this news, both feeling that God could continue to strengthen Dad for the work he had been called to do. That answer to prayer for strength was not forth coming. The headaches became so severe the doctor recommended an examination by a well-known neurologist. The results of this examination were tragic news. Dad had a clot in one of his neck arteries. He was given two choices—to have an operation with a greater possiblity of death or to be paralized for life unless he could retire immediately from the ministry.

Dad made his decision: Doctor, I'd rather die in the pulpit than retire or live the rest of my days in a wheelchair."

I wished I could talk to my father, but he seemed to be in another world, not wanting to talk, not wanting to read, not wanting to pray. "God, how can this be?" I wondered if Mother noticed Dad's behavior. I could not bring myself to even question her, but I could tell by the deep lines of grief, Mother was praying and was concerned.

Then at last I had my opportunity. Dad wanted me to drive him into the Poconos to his eye specialist. How well I remember his words: "Honey, I guess you've noticed I haven't been winning many victories lately. I don't know why I went through this dryness of soul, but I can tell you this, I've come through it all with a new and greater vision of the Lord. That dark veil has been lifted and I feel on the verge of a great victory."

That following Sunday Dad preached a sermon on heaven. "I'm looking forward to that day He comes in the clouds to take His bride home. It seems I can see Jesus standing there waiting for the Father to say, 'Now, my Son.' " I saw Mother, with tears streaming down her face. Mother knows of Dad's triumph too, I thought.

Mother was sensing something else. Dad had been close to death so many times, and now she was seeing him suffer again, such suffering as she had never seen before. She had watched and prayed in silence, only telling us in part of Dad's difficulties in balancing himself, in focusing his eyes and in thinking clearly. In her agony she wondered what kind of victory God had prepared for His servant.

Dad seemed to be much better. He wanted to talk, to visit with us, and to question us about our tentative plans for Don to enter the ministry. He radiated such joy we couldn't help notice he had won another victory.

A few days later he wrote to his friend, Gillam: "I don't seem to be able to hit those keys very well . . . that's been one of my problems since the accident . . . I can still shout the victory, and preach all over the church. And I can hold on to the pulpit and sing like an angel from heaven when I am annointed. I love fellowship, and this year has been hard on me—the children have been here, but I miss my buddy."

True friend that he was, Gillam was in Scranton a week later. I asked Gillam to tell me of his visit with Dad. "We visited together in the study. He told me about his hospital stay, all his trials during his sickness and the accident that had caused it all. He told me that when he was in the hospital for those weeks with only four walls to look at, his life seemed to him to be just one trouble after another. His body was not up to it. He prayed to die. (This shocked me.) One day the doctor came in and he asked him if he could go home. The doctor replied that he could see no reason why not, if he really wanted to go. Kenneth got the ball rolling and he went home. It was then that he wrote me. I replied that I could probably arrange to come over later in the spring. I think he called when he received my answer and asked me to come. This was quite sudden, but I felt I should arrange it and I did. He told me, 'Now that I am home, things look good to me. I look at everything, every stick of furniture. It all looks good to me and I want to live.' I took him to a doctor who, it was said, could help the severe pain in his head. He advised him not to have the nerve cut in his neck. Kenneth had already vetoed this idea. While I was with him, it became real to me how hurt he had been with the loss of equilibrium. He took hold of my arm as we walked, he took hold of the pews as he went down the church aisle and he held on to the pulpit when he talked. All this was noticeable, but I had no idea that it was serious.

"The visit was too brief but I have to get back. When I said goodbye, I thought he looked unusually well. Though it took him quite a while to get downstairs, he looked good."

Just three days after Gillam left, Mother called at our apartment and calmly said, "Ruth, I'm waiting for an ambulance. The doctor seems to think Dad has a virus, but I feel it is much worse."

I hung up the phone with a sense of foreboding and went into the living room to pray, but I could not. That still, small voice said, "Your father is not going to live. It's time for him to go home." I could not pray, I could only cry; neither could I comprehend at that moment the meaning of death. No one close to me had died: I had never experienced the awfulness of final separation upon this earth.

Two days later, on his way to work, my husband stopped to see Dad. Just minutes after his arrival he called the parsonage where we were now staying with Mother. "Ruth, your father is dead." It was only then that I knew what death was all about. In spite of my sorrow I could not forget the most wondrous part of death that Dad had dwelt on—Christ's victory over death and our eternal reward in heaven. That was Dad's faith. It was good enough for Father, and it's good enough for me. There is no other Way.

IT WAS GOOD
ENOUGH FOR
FATHER

With unpretentious simplicity, Ruth Wilkerson Harris traces the family history from Great-Grandfather to the present generation. Her own personal warmth and honesty are reflected as she tells the story of three generations of fiery Pentecostal preachers and their families.

J. A. Wilkerson started it all when he felt the call and stumbled down the church aisle. Consumed by tuberculosis, suffering from stomach ulcers, and limping on a game leg, he surrendered his arrogant, deceitful, stubborn life to God to do with as He pleased.

God took that life and used Grandfather Wilkerson in a mighty way as He called him to an evangelistic ministry, tested him, healed his ravaged body and permitted him to be the instrument whereby countless persons were reborn into a life of faith. A vehement preacher — zealous, dramatic, bombastic — he preached the old-time religion with fervor the rest of his life.

Among those converted under his preaching was his son Kenneth, a willful young man who at seventeen had joined the marines, disclaiming any of his religious heritage; but he reckoned without